Contents

Preface

After years of neglect, the Welfare State has now been moved to the forefront of examination syllabuses. This refects, of course, the media attention it is getting. And yet a chief examiner can write:

> 'There was remarkable confusion among candidates as to what actually constitutes the Welfare State.'

Whereas another, in his revised syllabus summary, is equally explicit:

> 'The operation of particular markets (has) typically been the subject of close attention by governments. These are the markets in education, housing and health care. This section is the subject of increased emphasis.'

The recent address that David Whynes gave to the annual meeting of the Economics Association, on the NHS, qualifies him to cover this poorly served part of the syllabus.

The second examiner quoted above gave the following example:

Health care –
  Identify the problem.
  What are society's objectives?
  How do governments currently attempt to achieve these objectives?
  What problems are likely to occur?
  Alternative solutions.

David Whynes answers all these questions for health, social security, education and housing.

Bryan Hurl
Series Editor

Acknowledgement

Grateful thanks are due to the many organizations who permitted me to reproduce material for which they hold the copyright. These include the *Guardian*, the *Independent*, the *Daily Telegraph*, the *Times*, the *Daily Mail* and the *Observer*. On a more personal note, Bryan Hurl provided generous assistance in the form of advice and comments on earlier drafts. My wife, Jane, graciously tolerated my writing commitments whilst caring for our new-born son, Benedict. To him, I dedicate this book – a small book for a small boy.

Chapter One
What is the Welfare State?

'A decent provision for the poor is the true test of civilization.'
Dr Samuel Johnson, Boswell's *Life*, 1770

Economists use the term 'welfare state' to refer to those social welfare services in the economy which are organized and provided by the government. In the UK, the four principal types of welfare service are:

- cash benefits concerned with the relief of poverty, arising from, for example, unemployment, sickness or old age – these benefits are generally referred to as SOCIAL SECURITY;
- public sector primary, secondary and higher EDUCATION;
- HEALTH CARE provided by the National Health Service (NHS), and related personal social services, such as residential care of the elderly and social work;
- public sector HOUSING, and cash benefits to assist individuals with housing costs.

The importance of the Welfare State in the modern UK economy can be gauged by the size of the claim it makes on both government and national resources. As may be seen from Figure 1, the Welfare State areas have together absorbed, on average and over the past two decades, slightly more than one-half (53 per cent) of government spending each year. Of comparable size to the health care and education allocation has been spending on national defence and the servicing of the national debt (interest payments on monies borrowed by the government from financial institutions). Each year, around one-quarter of public spending has also been allocated to a large number of other areas. None of these represents more than 3 per cent of the spending total, the majority far less. The areas include transport and communication, agriculture and industry, the police, the law courts, prisons, libraries, museums, public parks, refuse disposal, street lighting and the fire service. Since 1970, total government spending as a proportion of the gross national product (GNP) has averaged 43 per cent each year. It accordingly follows that, over the past two decades, the Welfare State has regularly accounted for 23 per cent of GNP per annum, between one-fifth and one-quarter of the entire economy.

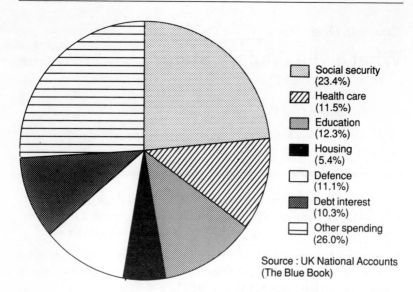

Figure 1 Average annual allocation of public expenditure since 1970

Clearly, this proportion represents a huge amount of resources, and another way of assessing the scale of the enterprise is to see where all the money goes. Here are some illustrations (bear in mind that the UK population is around 57 million individuals):

- As regards the allocation of cash benefits at present, there are approximately 4 million recipients of assistance with rent, rates and community charge bills, over 10 million recipients of state retirement pensions, over 4 million recipients of grants by virtue of low income, and over one million recipients of invalidity benefit.
- The UK government operates and maintains approximately 30 000 schools containing over 8 million pupils. It employs 450 000 teachers and a slightly smaller number of support staff. In addition, there are nearly half a million students in public higher education, taught by 125 000 teachers.
- Via the National Health Service, more than 8 million courses of hospital treatment are undertaken each year (along with more than 13 million accident and emergency cases). The NHS employs slightly in excess of one million people (half of whom are nurses), making it by far the biggest single employer of labour in the country, and one of the largest in Europe. Over 435 million NHS drug prescriptions are dispensed each year (equivalent to at least seven for every member of the population).

- Over 5 million homes in the UK (around one-quarter of the total housing stock) are owned and leased out by the public sector. Each year, more than 150 000 homeless families are found accommodation by local authorities.

The birth of the Welfare State

The man who in 1941 first coined the phrase 'welfare state' actually had in mind something far more broad than the definition given above. William Temple, the then Archbishop of York, used the term to describe the sort of society he hoped would be constructed after the end of the Second World War. This was to be an economy operating for the benefit of all its citizens, the very opposite of the totalitarian dictatorships of Hitler's Germany and Stalin's USSR. However, the term was popularly adopted to apply to social policy in the UK following a series of Acts of Parliament, all of which came into effect on 5 July 1948. These Acts created the National Health Service and established the basis of the current system of social security. Whilst significant in themselves, they built on and consolidated a very large body of welfare legislation which had been accumulating since Victorian times. Moreover, they completed the social welfare jigsaw, by complementing government policies for housing and education already in place. *Thus 5 July 1948 is the traditional birthday of the Welfare State.*

Editorial in *The Times*, 5 July 1948

Today the British people join together in a single national friendly society for mutual support during the common misfortunes of life. The coming into force of the National Insurance Acts completes the work begun by the friendly societies in the nineteenth century and carried further by compulsory social insurance in the twentieth. The National Insurance Act winds up half a millennium of social history by finally burying the Poor Law. The Assistance Board, the citizen's last defence against destitution, works according to rules which would have been unbelievable even forty years ago. The many other social services which have sprung from the Poor Law now go separate ways under new management, freed from the last lingering taints of "pauperism". The national health service, completely detached at last both from the Poor Law and from insurance, also begins today its more hazardous advance into a unknown future. The main outlines of a social service State approaching maturity are now plainly discernible in a logical array: the assumption by the state of a positive duty to prevent unavoidable idleness, ignorance, squalor, ill-health and want; the employment and training, insurance and assistance, hospital and general medical services nationally provided by three Ministeries with a variety of special managing bodies; all the most important remaining services for personal health, welfare, special accommodation, education, child care, and the planning of the physical environment concentrated in the hands of a new partnership of central with "major" local authorities. The new social security system is, as the Prime Minister said in his broadcast last night, the most comprehensive of its kind ever introduced into any country . . . In the maze and jumble of "post-war reconstruction" as it actually is, it would be a grave mistake to overlook the deep feelings and sense of purpose and common humanity which all the new social services are trying, however imperfectly, to express.

Studying the Welfare State

It is not too difficult to support the argument that the Welfare State is a most important topic for economists to study. To start with, as we have seen, the Welfare State is responsible for the allocation and distribution of almost one-quarter of the nation's resources. Second, the contemporary Welfare State impacts upon the lives of almost all British citizens, be they recipients of state pensions or other cash benefits, or users of public education, the National Health Service or public sector housing. The Welfare State is therefore a contributor to the standard of living of each and every one of us.

The 1980s witnessed the emergence of a protracted debate over the appropriate role and functioning of the Welfare State. Whilst some people appeared content to allow welfare services to continue to evolve in the way they had been doing over the previous four decades, others were not so sure. Some argued that welfare provision smothered individual initiative, and others suggested that it was all far too expensive. For its part, the UK government has, over the past decade, implemented major policy reforms in all the principal social welfare areas. Economists clearly have a role to play, both in contributing to the Welfare State debate and in identifying the strengths and weaknesses of the policy reforms.

This book is intended to provide a background to understanding the economic problems of, and the issues facing, the modern Welfare State. In the next chapter we shall examine some basic economic propositions relevant to the Welfare State in general, whilst the following four chapters deal in turn with the four main welfare areas – social security, education, health care and housing. The concluding chapter examines some of the Welfare State's current problems and assesses its prospects for the future.

SIR WILLIAM THE GIANT-KILLER

The Welfare State came into being as the result of the ideas and efforts of a great many people. However, if any one person can be identified as the principal architect of the Welfare State in Britain then it is surely **Sir William Beveridge** (1874–1964). Beveridge was a civil servant and a journalist turned academic, as Director of the London School of Economics between 1919 and 1937, and then as Master of University College, Oxford. He became a government advisor during the Second World War and, briefly, a Member of Parliament, before accepting a peerage and Liberal leadership in the House of Lords. To a greater or lesser extent, he made a contribution to every area of social policy which was implemented in the 1940s and 1950s.

Beveridge described the necessary road to social reconstruction after 1945 as an attack on five giants, whose names were 'Want, Disease, Ignorance, Squalor and Idleness'. The attack on ignorance was to be led by the 1944 Education Act, of which Beveridge was co-sponsor. Disease was to be defeated by the creation of the National Health Service. Idleness was to be overcome by the government's 1944 White Paper commitment to maintain 'a high and stable level of employment' by means of Keynesian economic management techniques. Squalor was to be addressed by the support of incomes, by housing development and by environmental planning. Beveridge's most sustained personal efforts were directed towards the attack on want, in the form of his book *Social Insurance and Allied Services*, published in 1942. Known to this day simply as the **Beveridge Report**, it laid the foundations of the modern system of unemployment and sickness insurance.

'Scrooge and Marley's, I believe,' said one of the gentlemen, referring to his list. 'Have I the pleasure of addressing Mr. Scrooge, or Mr. Marley?

'Mr. Marley has been dead these seven years,' Scrooge replied. 'He died seven years ago, this very night.'

'We have no doubt his liberality is well represented by his surviving partner,' said the gentleman, presenting his credentials.

It certainly was; for they had been two kindred spirits. At the ominous word 'liberality,' Scrooge frowned, and shook his head, and handed the credentials back.

'At this festive season of the year, Mr. Scrooge,' said the gentleman, taking up a pen, 'it is more than usually desirable that we should make some slight provision for the Poor and destitute, who suffer greatly at the present time. Many thousands are in want of common necessaries; hundreds of thousands are in want of common comforts, sir.'

'Are there no prisons?' asked Scrooge.

'Plenty of prisons' said the gentleman, laying down the pen again.

'And the Union workhouses?' demanded Scrooge. 'Are they still in operation?'

'They are. Still,' returned the gentleman, 'I wish I could say they were not.'

'The Treadmill and the Poor Law are in full vigour, then?' said Scrooge.

'Both very busy, sir?'

'Oh! I was afraid, from what you said at first, that something had occurred to stop them in their useful course,' said Scrooge. 'I'm very glad to hear it.'

'Under the impression that they scarcely furnish Christian cheer of mind or body to the multitude,' returned the gentleman, 'a few of us are endeavouring to raise a fund to buy the Poor some meat and drink, and means of warmth. We choose this time, because it is a time, of all others, when Want is keenly felt, and Abundance rejoices. What shall I put you down for?'

'Nothing!' Scrooge replied.

'You wish to be anonymous?'

'I wish to be left alone,' said Scrooge. 'Since you ask me what I wish, gentleman, that is my answer. I don't make merry myself at Christmas and I can't afford to make idle people merry. I help to support the establishments I have mentioned – they cost enough; and those who are badly off must go there.'

'Many can't go there; and may would rather die.'

'If they would rather die,' said Scrooge, 'they had better do it, and decrease the surplus population . . .'

[From *A Christmas Carol* by Charles Dickens]

Chapter Two

The economics of the Welfare State

'The State should do for the people what needs to be done, but which they cannot, by individual effort, do at all, or do as well for themselves.' Abraham Lincoln, 1860

Model of the market process

To find out why the Welfare State emerged and continues to this day, we have to step back a little way in history. Until the latter part of the nineteenth century, the government controlled only a small proportion of economic resources in industrialized societies. UK government spending was under 10 per cent of total output in the 1890s, less than one-quarter of today's share. Much of this was allocated to the provision of national defence and to the maintenance of law and order. Most resource allocation in the economy took place, as it had done for centuries, via the market. Drawing on this historical experience, economists have constructed an idealized model of the market process. The model, in essence, runs as follows.

In a market economy, individuals sell or rent out to others their productive resources – land, labour power, capital equipment, raw materials – in exchange for money incomes. These incomes enable them to buy from those other individuals – entrepreneurs or producers – who have employed such resources – factors of production – to generate consumable output. Consumers' expenditures thus become producers' revenues. In turn, these revenues are used in the further purchase of factors of production. Such purchase generates incomes for factor owners and the circle of exchange is completed, as illustrated in Figure 2. In this circle, prices and incomes are determined by the interaction of supply and demand. Thus, were supply greatly to exceed demand for, say, oranges and computer programmers, we should expect the price of oranges and the incomes of computer programmers to be relatively low, other things remaining equal. In the case of the oranges, moreover, the falling price of the product would induce the orange entrepreneur to attempt to lower costs, probably by reducing wages (incomes) of the orange pickers.

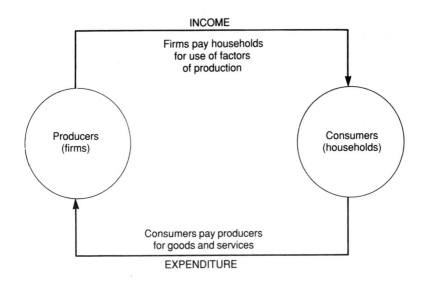

Figure 2 Circular flow of income and expenditure

Needless to say, the market remains the dominant allocation mechanism throughout much of the UK economy of today. However, over the past one hundred years, the status of the **government as an economic agent** has increased considerably. Indeed, the government is an unusual economic agent because, compared with most others, it is immensely powerful. As a legislator it is entitled to regulate exchange, for example, by prohibiting the trade of certain items or by ensuring that traded goods meet certain quality standards. Moreover, it possesses the legal power to tax the incomes and expenditures of all other economic actors, both consumers and producers, at rates set by itself. This means that it can cause the market price of goods to be raised or lowered by the imposition of an expenditure tax or subsidy.

The effects of taxes and subsidies on the market for a particular good are illustrated in Figure 3. For the given demand curve and producers' initial supply curve S_0, the market naturally clears at price P and quantity E. The effect of the imposition of a tax on output is to raise the supply curve vertically by the amount of the tax (BC) from S_0 to S_T. For all outputs, supply price is higher by the amount of the tax, and it is evident that the market now clears at price A and quantity T. Compared with the pre-tax equilibrium, price is higher and the quantity traded is lower. Total consumer expenditure (price multiplied by quantity) is given by the area ABTO, the producer's sales revenue is DCTO, and the government's tax revenue is ABCD.

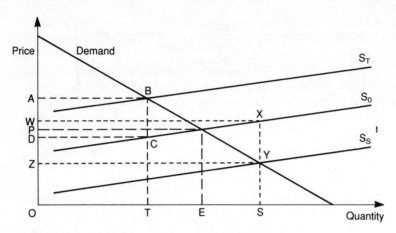

Figure 3 The effects of taxes and subsidies

The subsidy effect is completely symmetrical to the tax effect. With the same initial demand curve and supply curve S_0, the effect of a subsidy is to lower the supply curve vertically by the amount of the subsidy XY, from S_0 to S_S. For all outputs, supply price is lower by the amount of the subsidy, and the market now clears at price Z and quantity S. Compared with the pre-subsidy equilibrium, price is lower and the quantity traded is higher. The producers' sales revenue is now WXSO, comprising ZYSO obtained from consumers and a government subsidy to the value WXYZ. Accordingly, using a combination of taxes and subsidies, the government can restrict the consumption of commodities it feels people should consume less of, raise tax revenue for government expenditure purposes, or expand the consumption of commodities which it feels people should consume more of.

Income and expenditure taxes permit the government to effect income transfers between individuals. In principle, the government can take from the rich and give to the poor (or vice versa, for that matter). It is also empowered to act as an entrepreneur in its own right, purchasing factor inputs and providing outputs for sale, either at a price reflecting production costs or at a price subsidised by tax revenues.

With respect to the economic activities comprising the Welfare State, the UK government intervenes in all these ways. Specifically, it intervenes:

- By **regulation**. For example, it requires individuals in employment to make contributions to the National Insurance social security scheme and to pay income tax, it requires young people to attend school, and it ensures that only qualified physicians practise medicine.

- By **subsidy**. For example, it may offer public sector housing to families at less than the market rent, and drugs to NHS patients at a price well below the cost of production.
- By **public production**. In the cases of local authority housing and most of UK health care and education, the government is acting as the entrepreneur, hiring factors of production and making available the output to consumers, generally at a highly subsidised price. When consumers obtain welfare services at less than the market price they are said to be receiving **benefits in kind**.
- By **transfer payments**. Under the social security system, an amount of the revenue obtained from tax-payers is transferred to others – for example, pensioners, the unemployed, the sick, low-income families, single parents, households with children. With these **cash benefits**, recipients are free to buy goods and services of their choice at market prices.

Why does the government intervene?

It is evident that the government has considerable economic power, but why should it wish to wield it? The answer lies in the realization that the outcome of the market process in the economy is the result of a vast number of exchanges involving literally millions of decision makers. Each consumer makes up his or her mind about what to buy, from whom, and how much he or she is willing to pay. Similarly, each individual firm decides how many people, or how much capital, it wants to employ and the wage, or rate of interest, it is prepared to offer. Each individual transaction takes place when the buyer and the seller agree mutually acceptable terms. The final shape of the market economy as a whole, as it were, therefore derives from millions of exchange decisions, all of which are made in isolation from one another. *What makes sense to individuals, however, does not necessarily make sense to society as a whole.* Thus there is no guarantee that, overall, the system of market allocation is either:

- **efficient,** in the sense that, for a given supply of input resources, as many usable output resources as possible are being produced; or
- **equitable,** in the sense that all members of society feel that the resulting distribution of income between individuals is acceptable, fair or just.

Efficiency and equity are the two principal goals of all economic systems – economists assume that people would always prefer more to less from given resources, and that 'fair' is better than 'unfair'. Thus, in cases where efficiency and equity fail to be achieved as the result of the market process, the government may use its economic power to attempt to make the system more efficient and more equitable.

Intervention and efficiency

The specific reasons why many aspects of the Welfare State are more efficiently provided by governments will concern us in later chapters. However, in case it is doubted that individual decisions produce the most efficient outcomes for society, we shall consider an illustration.

Suppose that all education in the UK had to be bought from private schools. People value education for its intrinsic enrichment of their lives and for the increased wage or salary they can expect in later life as a result of being better qualified. Using the textbook market analysis, we know that the individual would purchase that amount of education where the expected **marginal benefit** gained from education equalled the school's **marginal cost** of provision. This is the amount Q_i in Figure 4, for which the individual would be charged a price P_i. As far as the individual is concerned, this is the right amount of education to buy.

However, education is an unusual commodity in that the education of each individual provides benefits to other members of society. Economists call these benefits **external benefits** (or **externalities**), because they accrue to people other than, in this case, the buyer and seller of education. Education, for example, is essential for communication, and without effective communication little in the economy could

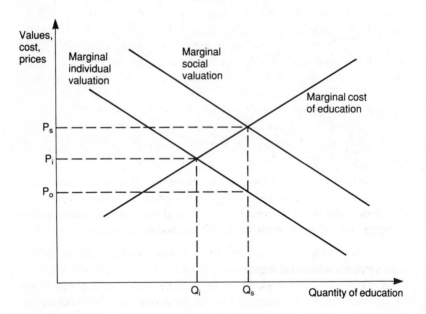

Figure 4 Optimum amount of education

be accomplished – think how many of the people with whom you come into regular contact rely on the fact that you have learned to speak and read English. Better educated parents produce income gains for their children. Educated people tend to be more flexible, thus accommodating more easily the stresses of social change and imposing fewer costs on their fellows.

Accepting the existence of these external effects, it is clear that society too will place a value on each individual's education, over and above the value placed by the individual himself. Thus in Figure 4 we can draw in a **marginal social benefit** of education at the various prices, to the right of the individual's marginal valuation. This marginal social benefit is the sum of the individual's marginal valuation and the additional social benefits mentioned above. Using the same market logic as before, but this time from society's rather than the individual's point of view, the optimum amount of education for the individual to purchase is Q_s, for which society is prepared to pay P_s. Now here is the problem. For society, the individual who buys Q_i education is not buying enough. However, to buy Q_s as society would like, the individual would only be prepared to pay P_o, a price too low to cover the school's costs.

From society's point of view, the private market has proved inefficient – it is not equating marginal social value with marginal cost. The resolution to the problem lies in the provision of a government subsidy to consumers of education. Assuming society is willing to pay for all the external benefits which it receives, the government (acting on society's behalf) can offer the individual money equivalent to the benefits. The government effectively says to the consumer: 'For every unit of education you buy, we'll give you spending power equivalent to the difference between your and society's benefits.' In Figure 4, this amount is represented by the vertical distance between the individual and social marginal valuations and is known as a **Pigouvian subsidy**, named after the Cambridge economist A.C. Pigou, who first suggested this solution. The individual's marginal value and that of society now become identical, the individual's value being determined by the personal benefits as before plus the subsidy offered by the government. With the subsidy, therefore, the individual rationally chooses to buy just the amount of education both he and society wants.

Intervention and equity

Table 1 displays the impact of taxes and benefits on UK households' market-determined income. The data are displayed for 'income quintiles', and quintile 1 refers to the average household income of the poorest 20 per cent of households in the country. Quintile 2 refers to

Table 1 Redistribution of market incomes (£) via taxes and benefits, 1987

	Household income quintiles				
	1	2	3	4	5
	(Poorest 20%)				(Richest 20%)
Market income	1220	3 850	9 470	14 510	25 470
Cash benefits	3 170	2 780	1 870	1 070	670
Gross income	4 390	6 630	11 610	15 580	26 140
Benefits in kind of which:	2 050	1 820	1 890	1 520	1 100
Education	800	660	840	630	360
Health care	1 030	980	920	790	630
Taxes	− 1 620	− 2 360	− 4 360	− 6 020	− 9 570
Final income	4 820	6 090	8 870	11 080	17 670

Source: Social Trends 21, Central Statistical Office, 1991

the average income of the next 20 per cent poorest, and so on up to quintile 5, the richest 20 per cent of households. Market income refers to earnings from employment, private pensions and investment. As may be seen, the richest households receive annual market incomes some 20 times those of the poorest households. Note, however, that as a result of taxation, cash benefits and benefits in kind, the distribution of final household income is much more even – the richest are now only 3–4 times as rich as the poorest, on average.

Information of this nature is often presented graphically as a **Lorenz curve**, and Lorenz curves for the UK are displayed in Figure 5. The Lorenz curve maps the proportions of total income received by proportions of the population, starting from the poorest households. The 'income equality' line maps out that which one would expect in theory if every household in the UK received the same income, and the further away is the Lorenz curve from this line then the greater the degree of income inequality. The 'market income' curve maps the distribution which would prevail if the UK were a **laissez-faire** economy (one in which the government neither taxed nor expended resources). As a result of the intervention which does take place, the 'final income' distribution clearly moves the economy towards more income equality.

The fact that such substantial redistribution takes place is clear proof that UK society regards the market-determined distribution of income as inequitable. Note that the poor, by and large, gain at the expense of

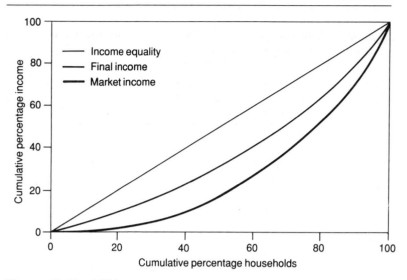

Figure 5 The UK Lorenz curve

the rich – the latter's final incomes in Table 1 are evidently less than their market incomes. One obvious explanation for the redistribution which takes place lies in the political system. A poor person may have less money than a rich one, but he has an equal number of votes. As is evident from Table 1, a substantial number of households, and therefore voters, are net beneficiaries of the Welfare State and presumably vote for political parties offering continuing or improved welfare services. Put another way, parties hostile to the Welfare State are likely to alienate much of their support and to jeopardize their electoral success.

Although rich people appear to lose out through income redistribution and the provision of welfare services, there are three reasons why they too might regard the Welfare State outcome as more equitable:

- Rich people may be **altruistic** and feel happier in the knowledge that the poor are being supported by their contributions. They may feel that society should guarantee a minimum living standard to all individuals as a matter of right.
- As eventualities such as unemployment, sickness, disability and old age are common to all individuals, the rich may be prepared to finance the provision of welfare services in these areas in case they themselves have need of such services in the future.
- Rich people might perceive that better housed, better educated and healthier poor people can make the economy more productive and more socially stable, and that it is worth paying for such productivity and stability.

The benefits in kind provided by the Welfare State are all **merit goods** – i.e. goods which would be under-supplied if left to normal market criteria. This under-supply is judged with reference to *both* efficiency *and* equity criteria. Thus education, health care or decent accommodation may be seen as merit goods because of the external benefits conferred by consumption (efficiency) and because society feels that all citizens should be entitled to a basic level of each (equity).

The dimensions of poverty

The relief of poverty is one of the principal objectives of the Welfare State. The eminent Victorian economist, Alfred Marshall, wrote that 'the study of poverty is the study of the causes of the degradation of a large part of mankind', the implication being that simple statistics of income distribution do not convey the true nature of poverty. Because income is the key to living standards in a market society, poverty tends to be at the root of a great variety of social problems.

Homeless youths 'turning to theft'

Growing numbers of homeless teenagers denied benefits are turning to thieving, drug pushing and begging, according to confidential research prepared for the Government.

The research by Mori, which MPs are allowed to see in the House of Commons library but not take away, was yesterday removed by Brian Wilson, Labour's Scottish Affairs spokesman, so he could denounce government handling of the homeless.

The report, based on interviews of 551 homeless 16- and 17-year-olds across Britain who had applied for severe hardship payments, reveals that one third of the men got money through begging, stealing and drug pushing, and one quarter of the women were pregnant.

Over half were sleeping rough, one in six had no money at all when they put in their hardship claim, and half had been thrown out by their parents. A minority were living in friends' homes and a few still could return to their parents.

One in five said they had been sexually abused by a relative or children's home staff, and one in 10 had been in care.

The report, which is marked Do Not Remove and was lent to the Guardian, shows that many of the teenagers were escaping debts. All those interviewed owed a minimum of around £20, 41 per cent owed over £100, and one in 20 £350 or more.

The research, published in the same month as the Government's Citizen's charter promising better treatment at benefit offices, is critical of the handling of young homeless by benefit office staff.

Where they had been turned down for severe hardship payments, the offices kept no record of what happened to them.

The research found that 84 per cent were kept waiting over an hour at benefit offices. Half were told the office could not find their file and many reported delays in receiving their girocheque once it was granted.

Non-whites were more likely to report delays in receiving cheques and being asked to return on unnecessary visits.

Referring to the Social Security Act, which in 1988 removed the right of 16- and 17-year-olds to claim benefits, Mr Wilson said: "There is not the slightest doubt that this act of Government, dreamt up when John Major was the responsible social security minister, has had the effect of putting thousands of vulnerable youngsters on to the streets and into despair."

"The research deals only with those who had enough knowledge to seek severe hardship payments which can be granted in exceptional circumstances. Even that concession had to be dragged out of the Government in the early days of the measure."

"This report should be hung round the neck of Citizen John as a memorial to his idea of a classless society."

The Department of Social Security has recently extended the right to benefit to a small number of 16- and 17-year-olds formerly in council care.

Source: *Guardian*, 26 July 1991

Poorest left behind in worst council housing, study says

Three council house tenants in four are reliant on state benefits, a new study of British housing shows. As those who can afford to do so move out, estates are increasingly populated only by the poor and the deprived. The study, *Paying for Britain's Housing*, blames poverty traps created by housing benefit and social security regulations from preventing thousands of the poorest people from breaking out of what Professor Duncan Maclennan, of Glasgow University, described as "the grimmest housing conditions". Large post-war council housing estates have become new centres of deprivation, the report shows. . . . Although unemployment has played an important part in causing deprivation on council estates, most claiming benefit were disabled, long-term sick, elderly or single parents. . . . Professor Maclennen said: "I cannot stress enough the extent to which there is benefit dependence among those who live in the social rented sector." The survey found that pensioners in council housing had virtually no assets, having spent all their savings, if they had any, before they retired.

Source, *The Times*, 4 December 1990.

Mother who robbed building society is freed from jail

A mother who turned to robbing building societies to support her family was yesterday ordered to be freed from her four-year jail sentence by the Court of Appeal. . . . Jones, who has twin daughters aged four, fell into debt after her husband was made redundant and then became ill. She also had to look after her father and diabetic young sister as well as running the family finances. The judge said: "By 1990 the finances were in a dreadful state. The family were threatened by the bailiffs and they risked their home being re-possessed." Jones, ill with glandular fever herself, did not want to burden her father and husband with the problems. After "veiled threats" from creditors, she became depressed and suicidal and turned to crime.

Source: *The Times*, 30 July 1991

Change in the Welfare State

From our discussions so far it is evident that the scope of the Welfare State is very extensive indeed. In one way or another, it impacts on the lives of just about everyone in the country. It is important to appreciate that the precise form of the Welfare State is always changing, and in two senses. First, and whilst it is fair to say that the basic agenda of social welfare was set by the legislation of and before 1948, governments are constantly experimenting with new methods of welfare delivery. Prior to 1979, for example, children represented a tax deduction against parental income – the larger the family the less the tax which the family had to pay.

This system was amended by abolishing these deductions and by replacing them with a flat-rate 'child benefit', a fixed weekly cash benefit paid to the family in respect of each child. There are currently more than 12 million children with parents receiving child benefit in the UK. Again, the 1948 pensions legislation – which provided for a fixed level of pension for all recipients – was drastically revised in 1975, with the intention of making the pension more closely related to the level of earnings during the individual's working life. Finally, since 1989, the National Health Service has been the subject of the most dramatic reform since its inception, intended to improve the efficiency of health care delivery. We shall consider later the economic wisdom of these sorts of changes, although it should be pointed out that few ever pass without a degree of political controversy. (Consider, for example, the reaction to the Conservative government's NHS reforms as evidenced by the *Guardian* extract, 'Doctors vote . . .'.)

Doctors vote to step up fight on health changes

Doctors yesterday attacked their chairman for taking a "softly softly" approach to the Government's health changes and voted to step up their public opposition to them.

Amid heated scenes at the British Medical Association annual conference in Inverness, doctors said that they did not want their leaders to be seen helping the Government to make the changes operate more smoothly. The National Health Service, they said, was not safe in the Government's hands. A number of delegates called for the resignation of Dr Jeremy Lee-Potter, chairman of the BMA council, after a lacklustre speech in which he said the medical profession and the Government should work together.

Dr Lee-Potter later told a press conference that he was fundamentally opposed to the health changes but did not see the point of "yah boo-ism".

He described statements that the NHS was not safe in the Government's hands as rhetoric. "Confrontation in public might salve people's feelings but it doesn't necessarily butter the parsnips at the end of the day." He said he was not considering resignation. "It is easy to get the impression that because I am personally not thumping tubs all the time that my intrinsic beliefs are not the same as

those who believe we should be tub thumping."

He added: "As far as the BMA is concerned, we have made some progress with the Government. I want to be inside the room talking with the Government, not outside shouting."

Earlier, the 600 delegates voted overwhelmingly that the NHS was not safe in the Government's hands, and that the BMA should campaign with more vigour to modify the health changes.

They condemned underfunding of the health service, saying the changes had not addressed this fundamental problem.

The doctors wanted to halt the second wave of opted out hospitals until the full effects of the first wave had been studied. They also said £6 billion was needed immediately to clear waiting lists and upgrade Victorian hospitals.

Dr John Rogers, a Bristol GP, said waiting lists were being swept under a bureaucratic carpet and were being renamed "pending lists" to make them sound more acceptable.

Dr Simon Fradd, a Nottingham GP, said the Government did not have the political will to ensure the health of the nation. "The only political will is to be elected. We have a responsibility as doctors to stand up for the people of Britain,"

he said.

Speaking later to journalists, Dr Fradd, a member of the BMA council, said he believed Dr Lee-Potter should either step up his public opposition to the health changes or resign.

Paddy Ross, chairman of the joint consultants committee of the BMA and the royal medical colleges, said the Government was bleeding an already anaemic NHS.

"The public is confused," he said. "We have a duty, irrespective of one's individual political allegiance, to give the public an unequivocal statement as to where the BMA stands."

In his speech, Dr Lee-Potter said doctors had to understand the Government's political position and work with the system they now had. "There have been recent signs that we can work together. Let us build on this."

However, he said the health changes were wasting money on administration that could have been spent on patients.

"The internal market will cost about £2 billion initially and its operating costs will be about £500 million annually for the next few years. You could buy an awful lot of care with that kind of money under the old system," Dr Lee-Potter said.

Source: *Guardian*, 2 July 1991

Ministers appeal for extra £15bn

Ministers have put in bids for close to £15 billion in extra cash for the next financial year, facing the Government with the prospect of a prolonged and bitter row over public expenditure this autumn.

This is 50 per cent above previous estimates of a £10 billion gap between the bids and the Treasury spending target.

Sharply rising unemployment, the cost of bringing down poll tax bills, and the need to finance politically sensitive areas such as health, education and transport before an election have meant that the Treasury is already privately admitting it cannot hope to keep the planning total for 1992-93 to the £215 billion set last November.

However, it has been made clear that the Treasury intends to go through the bids line by line to try to keep as close to the target as possible. "It will be bloody. There is no doubt about that," one source said.

Negotiations begin in August, after the Cabinet has discussed next year's public expenditure.

In recent years, the planning total has always overshot the original target after a long battle, but it is generally accepted that the election makes this year's negotiations even more crucial than usual. The Cabinet is expected to want to keep as close to the planning total as possible, leaving it to the Chief Secretary to the Treasury, David Mellor, to negotiate with individual ministers in the summer and early autumn.

Any disputes which have not been settled with him at the Conservative Party conference will go to the Star Chamber.

Mr Mellor is likely to receive strong backing from the Prime Minister and the Chancellor, who both made their reputations by adroit and tough handling of spending rounds.

Written bids arrived at the Treasury a month ago. Sources believe there is plenty of fat to be cut without affecting services. But the Government is not underestimating the political sensitivity, which is one reason why some Cabinet ministers still nurture hopes of an autumn election.

Treasury ministers argue that it would make a nonsense of Conservative attempts to brand Labour the party of high public spending if the Government loses its own grip on expenditure. Having recently claimed that immediately implementing all the Opposition's spending priorities would cost £35 billion a year, these ministers are keen to avoid an "own goal" when next year's total is revealed in the Autumn Statement. They are also concerned that the financial markets could be over-run, jeopardising further cuts in interest rates.

Spending ministers are basing their arguments on Labour's opinion poll lead over the Tories in issues such as health and education. They believe it would be playing into Labour's hands if Treasury frugality led to more hospital wards closing before a spring election.

Next year's planning total includes a £7 billion contingency reserve. The Treasury is likely to use at least half of this to fund higher spending. But, with every 100,000 on the unemployment roll adding £300 million to public expenditure and the poll tax subsidised, this will be quickly used up.

Source: *Guardian*, 8 July 1991

The second change in scope has to do both with the new policy initiatives and changing political priorities over time. Figure 6 shows the proportions of government spending devoted to the four major social welfare areas over the past two decades. As may be seen, social security constitutes by far the largest area of Welfare State spending, and its importance has increased particularly since the late 1970s. Housing's share of resources appears to be declining, whilst health care has recently overtaken education as the second-biggest recipient of public welfare spending. Incidentally, one consequence of regular policy changes in the Welfare State is the necessary re-definition of expenditure categories over time. The data in Figure 6 are a case in point. In 1981, the system of providing people with cash benefits to help them meet housing costs was overhauled. Since that date these 'housing benefits' have been included in the official social security budget, rather than in the housing budget as before. In order to present a consistent picture over time, however, Figure 6 continues to classify housing benefits under the housing budget (and excludes them from social security) after this date.

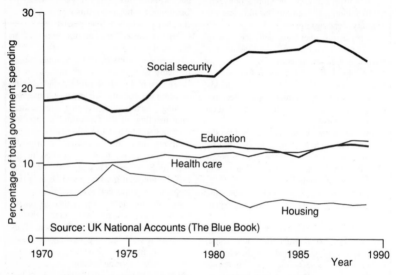

Figure 6 Government spending on the Welfare State

KEY WORDS

Government as an economic agent	Marginal cost
Regulation	External benefits
Subsidy	Externalities
Public production	Marginal social benefit
Benefits in kind	Pigouvian subsidy
Transfer payments	Lorenz curve
Cash benefits	Laissez-faire
Efficient	Altruistic
Equitable	Merit goods
Marginal benefit	

Reading list

Hurl, B., Chapter 2 in *Privatization and the Public Sector*, 2nd edn, Heinemann Educational, 1992.

Jenkins, S.P., 'Living standards and inequality', *Economic Review*, Jan. 1990.

Paisley, R. and Quillfeldt, J., Chapter 10 (Spending the taxpayer's money) in *Economics Investigated*, Collins Educational, 1992.

Wilkinson, M., Chapters 1 and 5 in *Efficiency and Equity*, Heinemann Educational, 1992.

Essay topics

1. Explain carefully the distinction between private benefits and social benefits. Describe and assess the measures which a government might take to increase a nation's welfare in cases where social benefit exceeds private benefit. (University of Cambridge Local Examinations Syndicate, 1989)
2. 'There are very good reasons why the government should supply certain goods and services not charged for by prices. The problem is that, unlike private firms selling goods in a free market, governments have little information regarding how much they ought to supply'. Discuss. (Welsh Joint Education Committee, 1987)
3. In what senses could the market system 'fail'? To what extent could your arguments be used to justify the production and distribution of goods by the public sector? (University of Oxford Delegacy of Local Examinations, 1989)
4. To what extent do supply and demand determine the provision of housing, health care and teachers? (University of London School Examinations Board, 1990) [note: This question is answered in *Economic Review*, September 1991]
5. Distinguish between wealth and welfare. Discuss whether increases in national income provide a suitable indication of improvements in welfare. (Associated Examining Board, 1987)

Data Response Question 1

Household income

This task is based on an examination question set by the University of Oxford Delegacy of Local Examinations in 1989. Study Table A which is derived from Social Trends 17 (HMSO) and, making use of your knowledge of economics, answer the questions.

Table A UK household income – national totals

	1975	1977	1979	1981	1983	1985
Income (percentages)						
Wages and salaries	69	67	66	64	62	60
Income from self-employment	8	9	8	8	8	9
Rents, dividends, interest	6	6	6	7	7	8
Private pensions, annuities, etc.	5	5	5	6	7	7
Social security benefits	10	11	12	13	13	13
Other current transfers	2	2	2	2	3	3
Total household income (£ billion)	88	112	153	201	238	283
Direct taxes, etc. (percentage of total household income)						
Taxes on income	17	16	14	14	15	15
National insurance contributions	3	3	3	3	4	4
Contributions to pension schemes	2	1	2	2	2	1
Total household disposable income (£ billion)	69	89	124	162	189	225
Real household disposable income per head (index numbers, 1980 = 100)	90	87	99	98	103	111

1. Describe the major economic trends that may be discerned from Table A.
2. What is meant by 'disposable income'?
3. Distinguish between 'cost of living' and 'standard of living'.
4. If you were attempting to estimate changes in the standard of living, which figures would you use, and why?
5. What further information would you require to assess accurately the changes in the standard of living?

Chapter Three

Social security

'Some day, perhaps, a statesman will emerge who will introduce a method and an order into the whole system. ... He might, if political circumstances and national finances allowed, be able to deal at one stroke with the three crying evils of invalidity, sickness and unemployment.' Harold Spender (journalist), 1909

We saw in the last chapter that the market system in the UK gives rise to substantial disparities in income, implying that families towards the bottom end of the income distribution would face the prospect of very low living standards indeed were government not to intervene. Why are such families poor? There are a number of potential explanations for poverty in market economies, the major ones being the following:

- Individuals will be poor if they are *unable to sell their labour* in exchange for money wages. Examples include people who cannot find an entrepreneur willing to employ them, people beyond the age of retirement, and the sick and disabled who are physically incapable of working.
- An employed individual can be poor if he is working in a *low-income occupation*. Wages in the market economy are determined with reference to the demand for and supply of labour, and the employer will pay his workers according to the value of output which each contributes. Suppose that the employer estimates that one additional worker will enable 10 more units of output to be produced by the factory each week, units which may be sold at a market price of £3 per unit. The new worker's **marginal revenue product** (the value of his contribution to output) is thus £30 per week. This figure sets the amount that the employer would be willing to pay the worker. To pay him more than he contributes would not be economic, and would entail the employer subsidizing the employee out of the profits of the enterprise. Generally speaking, firms are run on commercial rather than charitable lines, so the fact that a wage of £30 per week means the employee is poor by national standards is of no concern to the employer.

- Households will be poor if these exists a *large number of dependants* with respect to each principal bread-winner. The average individual income of a married couple, with one partner earning £180 per week and supporting both, amounts to £90. Were this household also to contain three children and an elderly relative, however, average income would fall to £30 per week. The far higher level of spending entailed by care of the four dependants would reduce the couple's standard of living very considerably.
- A family may be considered poor if it is faced with a *relatively high level of unavoidable expenses*. The payment of income and local authority taxes is a legal requirement. The non-payment of rent will lead to eviction, and long-term survival without heat and light is an unpleasant experience for most. Bills such as these simply have to be met. The amount of money involved could well represent a considerable proportion of household income, leaving very little for the purchase of other goods and services. Single parents particularly fall into this expenses trap – in order to go out to work they are obliged to pay others to care for their children.

Basic principles

The purpose of social security benefits is to alleviate household poverty which results from any or all of the above reasons, by augmenting household income with additional cash benefits. The principles of social security in the UK are extremely straightforward and rely only on a few basic ideas. Unfortunately, the operation of the system in practice is mind-bogglingly complex, as we shall see shortly. However, let us begin by considering some of the fundamental concepts.

All individuals pay income tax at the statutory **marginal tax rate** on market incomes exceeding a given **tax threshold**. For individuals whose incomes fall below this threshold, no tax is paid. However, certain of the social security benefits available are regarded as additions to market income and thus liable for taxation if the threshold is reached. This basic income tax mechanism is illustrated in Figure 7.

The many different cash benefits available within the social security system are all **categorial benefits**. In other words, in order to qualify for a certain benefit your circumstances have to accord with the definition of the appropriate category. Thus only those people registered as disabled are entitled to Disability Benefit. Only males over 65 years of age (and females over 60) are entitled to a State Pension. Only those families with incomes and savings below specified levels are eligible for Family Credit.

The social security budget actually derives from two sources. One of

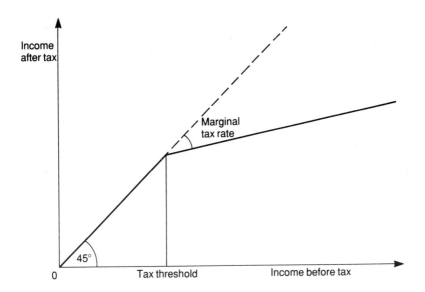

Figure 7 The income tax threshold

these is the **National Insurance Fund,** which finances **contributory benefits.** During the individual's working life he or she makes regular contributions to his fund – for the great majority of employees the National Insurance is automatically deducted from wages along with income tax. The contribution rate is related to earned income (people earning higher incomes pay proportionately more), and the worker's employer also make an equivalent contribution on his or her behalf. The individual may draw on this fund when unavailable for work – from this fund come, for example, sickness benefits, unemployment benefits and retirement pensions. The amount of benefit available depends upon the recipient's contribution record, a statutory minimum number of contributions being necessary for the receipt of full benefit. Note that this full benefit is **flat-rate** (i.e. invariant to previous income), although where the minimum contribution record has not been achieved reduced benefits are available.

The second source of cash benefits is the **Consolidated Fund,** which is really the Treasury's general coffer into which all tax and other revenues go. No contribution record is necessary in order to receive these benefits – all that is necessary is that the individual fulfils the correct categorical conditions.

Certain of the non-contributory benefits are **means-tested.** In such cases, the value of the benefit received by the individual or the household depends on the level of their market income, their wealth and their outstanding financial commitments. Only the poorest recipients obtain the full benefit. Less poor families have the value of the benefit reduced, up to a point where the recipient is deemed insufficiently poor to be eligible.

Who gets what?

Table 2 provides an expenditure breakdown of the social security budget by major benefit headings. It also gives an estimate of the current number of recipients of each type. Benefit categories are not exclusive to individuals, it should be remembered, so the same individual can be the recipient of more than one benefit. Many of these categories are

Table 2 Social security benefits, 1989–90

	Amount (£m)	Percentage of total	Recipients (thousands)
National Insurance (contributory) benefits			
Retirement pensions	20 802	40.0	9 710
Widow's benefit	916	1.7	400
Unemployment benefit	812	1.6	600
Sickness benefit	206	0.4	105
Invalidity benefit	3 890	7.5	1 100
Disablement benefit	471	0.9	325
Statutory sick pay	1 051	2.0	365
Statutory maternity pay	273	0.5	80
Other contributory benefits	302	0.6	
Sub-total contributory benefits	*28 723*	*55.2*	
Non-contributory benefits			
Child benefit	4 591	8.8	12 010
Single-parent benefit	204	0.4	705
Family credit	435	0.8	280
Income support	7 585	14.6	4 310
Attendance allowance	1 157	2.2	730
Mobility allowance	780	1.5	560
Invalidity pension/disablement allowance	331	0.6	270
Housing benefit	4 611	8.9	4 090
Other non-contributory benefits	1 020	2.0	
Sub-total non-contributory benefits	*20 714*	*39.8*	
Cost of administration	2 583	5.0	
Total social security expenditure	52 020	100.0	

Source: Social Trends 21, Central Statistical Office, 1991

self-explanatory, but some may require one or two words of explanation. As may be seen, all the contributory benefits relate to various reasons for temporary or permanent unemployment – retirement, death of working partner (in the case of wives with no contribution record), illness, disability, maternity. The 'unemployment benefit' as such is reserved for those seeking work and with a complete contributions record, although it is only available for a maximum period of 12 months. In the non-contributory categories, 'attendance allowance' is paid to elderly, infirm or disabled persons who require the occasional or constant assistance of others with the tasks of daily living. 'Mobility allowance' subsidizes the transport costs of those who find mobility difficult.

'**Income support**', one of the three major means-tested non-contributory benefits, is the principal form of cash assistance for adults whose market incomes and savings lie below government-defined levels. This is the benefit received, for example, by the unemployed who have no National Insurance contribution record. In principle, the claimant will receive a benefit equal to the difference between his or her market income (if any) and the defined level. In practice, however, the calculation is considerably more complicated, because age, martial status, other benefits received, mortgage repayments (if appropriate) and other housing expenses are also taken into account in determining the appropriate amount of benefit. This government-defined level is often referred to as the **poverty line**, the intention being that no individual should have a gross income lower than this amount.

'**Family credit**' is the parallel benefit system for the families of low-income, full-time workers. A comprehensive audit of family needs and income is undertaken and, if it is found that the family is worse off than it would be when assessed on the same basis as for income support, a government-determined maximum family credit is made available. However, for family incomes above the income-support assessment level, credit is withdrawn at a fixed rate, or **taper**. At the current rate of 70 per cent, therefore, for every £1 the family earns above the assessment level, 70 pence in benefit is lost. The principle of a benefit taper is illustrated in Figure 8.

'**Housing benefit**', which replaced the older system of rent and rates rebates, has been designed to be compatible with the other two means-tested benefits. Anyone at or below the income support level receives the full government-determined amount, and for incomes about this level the benefit is again tapered (currently at 80 per cent).

'**Child benefit**' is the principal non-means-tested, non-contributory benefit. Compared with the above, the mechanism of entitlement is

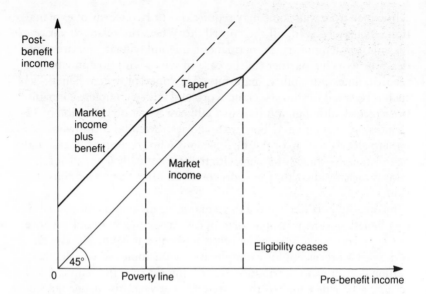

Figure 8 Benefit taper

simplicity itself. All parents, irrespective of their incomes, may simply draw a fixed amount each week in respect of each of the children for whom they are responsible.

The 'other' categories in Table 2 refer to literally dozens of smaller benefits which are available to claimants with specific poverty problems. However, it is worth noting that just five of the benefits noted in the table – retirement pensions, invalidity benefit, child benefit, income support and housing benefit – together account for 80 per cent of the total social security budget.

From Table 1 in the previous chapter, it is evident that, amongst the poorer households in the UK, social security benefits are very significant determinants of gross income. The table indicates that, for the poorest quintile, benefits account for 72 per cent (almost three-quarters) of gross income. The proportion is 42 per cent for the next poorest quintile, and both quintiles receive more in cash benefits than they pay in taxes. Now, the amount of every benefit to which any given citizen may be entitled is a matter for government discretion – we have already seen, for example, that the income support entitlement is made with reference to a government-defined level. Moreover, the government is also at liberty to vary whenever it wishes the contribution rates for National Insurance, to adjust the extent of the tapers of the means-tested benefits, and to vary the criteria for benefit eligibility. From all

this we can conclude that the incomes of the poorer part of the population are principally determined by whatever levels, rates and criteria the government happens to choose.

Each year, the official *Family Expenditure Survey* (FES) examines the income and expenditure patterns of a representative sample of UK households, and from such information we can obtain an idea of who the poorest people in our society really are. Table 3 displays the composition of the poorest quintile in the UK, measured as gross income and derived from FES data. It is evident that more than three-quarters of the poorest individuals in the UK are in the households of pensioners, the unemployed or workers receiving low wages. Indeed, more than one-half of all those living in families where the principal breadwinner is either unemployed or a single parent fall into the lowest income quintile. This leads us to an obvious but nevertheless important conclusion, namely, that it is predominantly the people receiving state benefits who are the poorest in society. Thus in spite of receiving all the cash transfers, *the poor both before and after the distribution of cash benefits tend to be one and the same.*

Table 3 Composition of the poorest 20 per cent of the population, 1987

Head of household	Individuals living in such households (millions)	Individuals in all such households (%)
Pensioner	2.7	29
Full-time worker	2.8	8
Sick or disabled	0.5	35
Single parent	1.0	54
Unemployed	2.9	59
Other	0.9	31
	10.8	

Source: *Households Below Average Income: A Statistical Analysis 1981–87*, Department of Social Security, 1990

Are the poor getting poorer?

We have established that the government is in control over the most important parameters of the social security system. If it so wished, one presumes, it could make far more generous provision for the poor, for example, by increasing the benefit levels to pensioners and to the unemployed. Actually, there is good evidence from successive *Family Expenditure Surveys* that the reverse has been taking place in recent years, and that the poor have been getting relatively poorer. Between 1981 and 1987, the average final incomes of the poorest 20 per cent of the population rose by 7–9 per cent. For the next poorest 30 per cent, the income rise was 10–15 per cent, although for the population as a whole, final income rose by 21 per cent. This must mean that the incomes of the richest half of the population have been accelerating away from those of the 30 per cent group who, in turn, are drawing away from the very poorest quintile. *Increases in benefits for the poor have clearly not kept pace with the increasing incomes of the rich*, and income distribution during the 1980s has gradually become more unequal. Indeed, the FES data show that, by 1987, 14 per cent of the population, and 20 per cent of all dependent children, were in households with less than half of the average UK income, as compared with 8 and 14 per cent, respectively, in 1981.

Depending upon your politics, you might consider that, on this evidence, the government has been acting either rightly or wrongly. Whatever your views, however, the determination of the possible

THE DISTRIBUTION OF HOUSEHOLD INCOMES DURING THE 1980s

The annual Family Expenditure Surveys collect data on gross (pre-tax) average household incomes for the UK population. The data are presented for ten 'deciles' – i.e. the average income of the poorest 10 per cent (decile 1), that of the next poorest 10 per cent (decile 2), and so on. Deflating the annual income figures by the retail price index (RPI) converts them into real average incomes. The graph shown here plots real average household incomes at 1989 prices for population deciles 1 (lowest line) to 9 (highest line). As may be seen, the lines gradually move apart over the time period, indicating that it is the higher-income households which have experienced the higher rates of income growth. By implication, income disparities between high– and low-income households have increased. Note that data for the highest income decile are not presented. The extreme income range of the most affluent UK households – varying between tens of thousands and many hundreds of thousands of pounds per year – makes an 'average' figure misleading in this case.

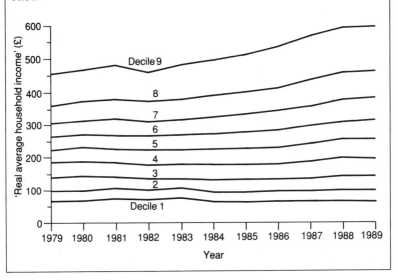

extent of redistribution via taxes and benefits results from a very complicated equation, as we shall now see.

In Chapter 2 we noted that the allocation of public spending is determined by political bargaining between the various spending arms of government. Given that the spending departments are bargaining for resources from the fixed Treasury 'pot', a solution might be to persuade the Treasury to increase the size of this pot. This could be accomplished by increasing taxation, for example, by raising the marginal tax rates on income tax, or the rate of value added tax (VAT). Raising taxes, however, is problematic, and is not a course of action governments happily contemplate. First, it is unpopular amongst taxpayers, who comprise a substantial proportion of the electorate. Second, tax increases are inflationary. An expenditure tax rise would be transmitted directly into a rise in the retail price index. A higher rate of income tax would leave taxpayers with lower real incomes, and could encourage them to bargain for higher wages.

Other elements of the equation are specific to the category of poverty being considered. Let us first examine the question of cash supplements to low-income families which, given the data in Table 3, appear to make up around one-quarter of the poorest quintile in the population. In this case, changes in benefit and tax levels have important **incentive** effects.

The unemployment trap

Suppose we rank households receiving employment income from high to low. For households towards the bottom of the distribution there will come a point where the disposable (post-tax) family income which it receives as a result of the bread-winner's working efforts actually equals the household's benefit entitlement under social security criteria. This, it should be mentioned, is by no means an implausible assumption. Average manual wages in 1990 were approximately £150 per week, whilst income support guaranteed a couple with two young children approximately £90 per week, plus access to full housing benefit. Beyond this cut-off point, we should presume that the rational household would leave the labour market and subsist on social security (on the assumption that leisure is preferred to work, other things remaining equal).

The model is shown in Figure 9. In the economy there are OP households, with incomes distributed along YP. For a social security benefit level of PB_1, ON_1 households will have employed bread-winners, whilst N_1P will prefer to exist on cash benefits (as their benefit income exceeds their disposable market income). Now suppose that the level of benefit is increased to PB_2. Clearly, the households who before found it *just* more profitable to obtain income from employment will now opt for unemployment and the receipt of benefits. The number of households in the economy with employed bread-winners will fall to ON_2. Further suppose that, in order to pay for the increased benefits, the

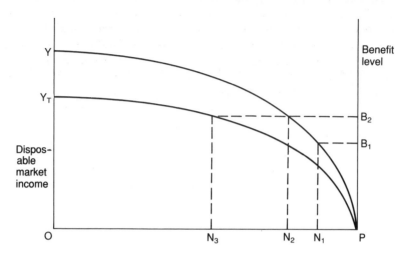

Figure 9 Incentive effects of benefit and tax changes

government elects to raise the level of taxation. Whilst the level of benefits remains the same, disposable market incomes for all households will fall, as distributed along $Y_T P$. In consequence, still more households who were on the margin of preferring employment to unemployment will opt for social security, and the level of employment in the economy will fall further, to ON_3. We conclude that both higher benefit levels and higher tax burdens encourage low-income households at the margin to leave the labour force. In addition to reducing aggregate production in the economy, the increase in unemployment will represent an additional burden on the existing social security budget. Now study Table 4 which applies this theory to current reality.

Retirement pensions

The UK pension system is an example of the **pay-as-you-go** (PAYG) schemes common in Western Europe. PAYG is to be contrasted with the private pension schemes which are available in the UK. These are **funded pensions** and, under a funded scheme, you make regular contributions into your own account, as it were, during your working lifetime. The fund is invested on your behalf, accumulates interest and is available for you to draw on during your retirement. A funded scheme is thus a method whereby the individual transfers money from

Table 4 The unemployment trap

Out of work		In work (stacking shelves in supermarket)	
Former earnings	£120.00	Gross earnings	£120.00
Unemployment benefit	£66.95	Tax	(£5.89)
Family credit	£26.41	National insurance	(£7.16)
Child benefit	£16.75	Child benefit	£16.75
Rent rebate	£18.26	Rent rebate	£0.00
Comm charge benefit	£5.73	Comm charge benefit	£0.00
		Travel to work	(£8.00)
Net income	£134.10	Net income	£142.11

Based on married couple with children aged 4 and 6

himself in the present to himself in the future. By contrast, under a PAYG scheme, the National Insurance contributions which you make today are being used to pay today's pensioners. When you come to retire at some point in the future, your pension will be financed by the contributions of the workers and employers of the future.

It therefore follows that increases in the level of pensions for retired people will require increasing contribution levels either from employees and employers, or possibly from both. Raising the levy on employers gives rise to unfortunate possibilities, because of the effect of increasing production costs. Employers may therefore be obliged to reduce output. Alternatively, they may demand less of the factor of production which has suddenly become more expensive and move into a labour-saving technology. In either case, increased unemployment could result. Even assuming that the employer does not shed labour, increased costs will have to be passed on to the consumer in the form of higher prices. Rather more success might be expected from raising employee contributions. Increasing National Insurance contributions is not so politically damaging as raising taxes, it seems, because (and in spite of what we have just learned above) a great many people think that they are paying for 'their' pension. Higher contribution rates might actually turn out to be popular politically, if the voters see this as the government promising better provision for their, the voters', old age. Better provision might well be the government's long-term goal, although in the short run it is simply liberating more funds for current pension payouts.

Is social security efficient?

Having decided on the form and extent of redistribution, the government enacts its proposals via the appropriate social security administrative procedures. It is therefore pertinent to ask: are these procedures efficient, in the sense of ensuring that the right people receive the right benefits at minimum cost? There are grounds for believing that this is not always the case in the UK.

To begin with, the claiming of benefits is administered in a quite different manner from the payment of taxes. Virtually all employees in the UK are within the **pay-as-you-earn** (PAYE) tax system, first introduced during the Second World War. Under PAYE, the employer deducts income tax and National Insurance contributions, as and when wages or salaries are paid. In a sense, therefore, your taxes are paid automatically on your behalf. By contrast, the benefit system places the onus on the claimant – *you will only receive a benefit if you actually register a claim*. On the basis of its own surveys, the Department of Social Security estimates that, for virtually all benefits, a proportion of those entitled to claim actually do not. Although the take-up for child benefit is close to 100 per cent, one in ten, it appears, does *not* claim income support, one in four does not claim housing benefit, and more than one in three fails to claim family credit. Clearly, the implication of non-take-up of benefits is that there are many people in the economy who are poorer than they actually need be.

Not claiming a cash benefit to which one is entitled appears, at first sight, to be distinctly irrational. So what are the reasons for non-take-up?

- Because the onus is on the individual to discover whether a benefit exists to which he or she might be entitled, some do not claim because they have *no knowledge of their entitlements*.
- Often the claiming procedure is *complex* – for example, the various rules about eligibility, means-testing and tapers. Long and difficult forms may have to be filled in, and a considerable amount of personal information may have to be provided, relating to income, family circumstances and housing tenure. In claiming for several different benefits, claimants may have sequences of interviews with several different officials.
- Certain individuals may be discouraged from claiming owing to the **stigma** attached to the receipt of state benefits. Low-income families entitled to free school meals for their children, for example, have been known to decline the benefit for fear of their children being thought 'paupers'. The widespread publicity given to benefit 'scroungers' and supposedly-unemployed 'moonlighters' may lead

to a fear of guilt by association on the part of potential claimants. To some, the claiming of benefit might be interpreted as uncomfortable evidence of economic inadequacy.

The poverty trap

We noted earlier that social security benefits might deter people from entering employment, if benefit levels were similar to expected wages. However, the present system also appears to allow little potential at the margin for a working individual to improve his circumstances by extra effort. Consider the case of a low-paid worker entitled to both family credit and housing benefit. Suppose he contemplated putting in a little extra effort at his job to earn an additional £1 per week. What happens to this extra £1? First of all, the value is reduced by around 34 pence in income tax and National Insurance contributions. The remaining 66 pence affects entitlement to family credit which has a 70 per cent taper; i.e. by earning 66 pence in market income, the worker loses 70 per cent of the amount (46 pence) in family credit, leaving him with 20 pence. Next, this 20 pence in earnings affects his housing benefit entitlement. Housing benefit has an 80 per cent taper; i.e. he loses 16 pence in

The room in which the boys were fed, was a large stone hall, with a copper at one end: out of which the master, dressed in an apron for the purpose, and assisted by one or two women, ladled the gruel at meal-times. Of this festive composition each boy had one porringer, and no more – except on occasions of great public rejoicing, when he had two ounces and a quarter of bread besides. The bowls never wanted washing. The boys polished them with their spoons till they shone again; and when they had performed this operation (which never took very long, the spoons being nearly as large as the bowls), they would sit staring at the copper, with such eager eyes, as if they could have devoured the very bricks of which it was composed; employing themselves, meanwhile, in sucking their fingers most assiduously, with the view of catching up any stray splashes of gruel that might have been cast thereon. Boys have generally excellent appetites. Oliver Twist and his companions suffered the tortures of slow starvation for three months: at last they got so voracious and wild with hunger, that one boy, who was tall for his age, and hadn't been used to that sort of thing (for his father had kept a small cook-shop), hinted darkly to his companions, that unless he had another basin of gruel *per diem*, he was afraid he might some night happen to eat the boy who slept next him, who happened to be a weakly youth of tender age. He had a wild, hungry eye; and they implicitly believed him. A council was held; lots were cast who should walk up to the master after supper that evening, and ask for more; and it fell to Oliver Twist.

The evening arrived; the boys took their places. The master, in his cook's uniform, stationed himself at the copper; his pauper assistants ranged themselves behind him; the gruel was served out; and a long grace was said over the short commons. The gruel disappeared; the boys whispered each other, and winked at Oliver; while his next neighbours nudged him. Child as he was, he was desperate with hunger, and reckless with misery. He rose from the table; and advancing to the master, basin and spoon in hand, said: somewhat alarmed at his own temerity:

'Please sir, I want some more.'

The master was a fat, healthy man; but he turned very pale. He gazed in a stupefied astonishment on the small rebel for some seconds, and then clung for support to the copper. The assistants were paralysed with wonder; the boys with fear.

'What!' said the master at length, in a faint voice.

'Please, sir,' replied Oliver, 'I want some more.'

[From *The Adventures of Oliver Twist* by Charles Dickens]

housing benefit. As a result of his additional labours, therefore, our worker has ended up with a 4 pence increase in gross income. In effect, this worker has faced a marginal tax rate of 96 per cent, a rate not conducive, one would think, to putting in the extra effort in the first place.

This is an example of the **poverty trap**, circumstances where increases in market incomes produce only minimal changes in net income owing to taxation and benefit reductions. Even more extreme is the case of part-time workers eligible for income support. In such cases, an extra £1 in earned income leads to an automatic withdrawal of £1 in benefit; i.e. a marginal tax rate of 100 per cent. Working in such circumstances produces precisely zero pecuniary advantage. Both these cases should be compared with richer workers with incomes well beyond the benefit entitlement levels, who can expect at least 60 pence in disposable income from every extra £1 earned.

The reform of social security

As you might expect, economists have not been slow in advancing ideas for social security reform, to overcome the sorts of problems discussed above. One of the best-known is the **negative income tax** (NIT), originally suggested by Milton Friedman in the 1960s. Under this scheme, all the many individual cash benefits would be superseded by a single benefit related to market income, which would then be integrated into the tax system. For each individual, a tax threshold would be defined, determined by, for example, marital status and family size. Broadly speaking, individuals with more dependants would have higher thresholds. The basic logic of the NIT approach is portrayed in Figure 10. At present, an individual in the UK pays no tax on incomes below his tax threshold, T, and then pays a proportion, r, on incomes above this amount. This is represented by the line OTY. Under the NIT system, the individual is guaranteed cash benefits OG for zero earned income, the benefits available being reduced by the same rate, r, for incomes between zero and T. The entire redistribution (both taxes and benefits) system is now automated – if your income is above T, you pay the government; if it's below, the government pays you. For example, with T set at £5000 and r at 25 per cent, individuals with incomes of £6000 pay £250 in tax, whilst individuals with incomes of £4000 receive £250. No-one falls below the guaranteed income minimum (£1250 in this case) and, given the constant marginal tax rate, no effort-disincentive poverty traps are created. Furthermore, the fact that everyone is in the scheme should resolve the earlier problem of claimant stigma.

Needless to say, such a scheme has not so far been implemented on a national scale. Whether NIT would involve a necessary increase in cost

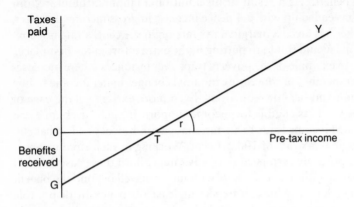

Figure 10 Negative income tax

remains a controversial point, although the answer clearly depends upon the chosen level of guaranteed income. In Figure 10, it can be seen that a larger guaranteed benefit at zero income would require a higher marginal tax rate for a given tax threshold. More complex NIT variants allow for the possibility of steeply progressive income taxes at higher incomes, which would permit a lower basic rate of tax/benefit redistribution, other things remaining equal. Certainly, such a radical overhaul of social security as envisaged by NIT would, in itself, be costly and time-consuming. Moreover, the NIT scheme poses one particular political problem for the government – in making the entire structure of benefits automatic, it actually removes one whole area of policy discretion from its own hands.

KEY WORDS	
Marginal revenue product	Taper
Marginal tax rate	Housing benefit
Tax threshold	Child benefit
Categorical benefits	Incentive effects
National Insurance Fund	Unemployment trap
Contributory benefits	Pay-as-you-go
Flat-rate	Funded pensions
Consolidated Fund	Pay-as-you-earn
Means-tested	Stigma
Income support	Poverty trap
Poverty line	Negative income tax
Family credit	

Reading list

Borooah, V.K., 'Poverty', *Economic Review*, Nov. 1991.

Jenkins, S.P., 'Living standards and inequality', *Economic Review*, Jan. 1990.

Johnson, P., 'Measuring poverty', *Economic Review*, Nov. 1990.

Paisley, R. and Quillfeldt, J., Chapter 13 (Signing on), Chapter 26 (Advancing years) and Chapter 29 (Rags and riches), in *Economics Investigated*, Collins Educational, 1989.

Stowell, G., 'Analysing taxes and benefits (exercise)', *Journal of the Economics Association*, spring 1991.

Terry, N.G., 'The changing UK pension system', *National Westminster Bank Quarterly Review*, May 1988.

Essay topics

1. Why have inequalities in the distribution of income and wealth increased in the UK in recent years? (Associated Examining Board, 1989)

2. Compare the advantages and disadvantages of (a) reducing income tax, (b) subsidizing incomes through cash benefits, (c) subsidizing the prices of goods and services, as methods of reducing poverty. (Associated Examining Board, 1989)

3. Examine fiscal policy as a means of redistributing income. (University of London School Examinations Board, 1988)

4. 'The United Kingdom's taxation and welfare benefits systems have trapped the low-waged in relative poverty and the un-waged in unemployment.' Explain the causes of this situation. Explain how problems created by this situation might be reduced. (Associated Examining Board, 1991)

5. What are the arguments for and against the view that standards of living in Britain are rising? Support your arguments with evidence. (Oxford & Cambridge Schools Examination Board, 1989)

Data Response Question 2

Poverty in Britain

This task is based on an examination question set by the Oxford & Cambridge Schools Examination Board in 1990. Read the following two passages and answer the questions.

1. Fabian Society, 1989

'Poverty in Britain has increased sharply since 1979, and a growing proportion are long-term poor. By 1985 (the latest available figures), 9.4 million people, including 2.25 million children, were living at or below the official poverty line. This is 17% of the population, an increase of 55% since 1979. In 1985, over 15 million people were living in poverty or on its margins (up to 40% above the Income Support scale. This is 28% of the population. In 1989, half a million families are caught in the poverty trap. For a couple with two children, if gross weekly earnings rise from £30.40 (when Housing Benefit starts to fall) to £165.90 (when Family Credit runs out), net income only rises from £126.20 to £143.70. An earnings rise of £135.50 increases net income by only £17.50. The effect of means-tested benefits is equivalent to a marginal tax rate of 87% over the whole income range.'

2. Conservative Party Research Department, 1989

'Are the poor "getting poorer"? No, they are not. It is clear that people at all income levels now have substantially more money to spend in real terms than they did in the 1970s. In fact, by almost every material measure it is possible to contrive – health, longevity, real income, ownership of consumer durables, number and length of holidays, money spent on entertainment, numbers in further education – not only are those with lower incomes not getting poorer, they are substantially better off than they have ever been before. Strong economic growth, coupled with cuts in income tax, have helped raise living standards to record levels. For a family with two children in the bottom 10% of the earnings league, real take-home pay has risen by almost 14% since 1979. The real incomes of the poorest tenth of the whole population rose by 8.3% between 1981 and 1985. Total spending on benefits has now increased by 33% in real terms since 1978/9.'

1. Define (a) the official poverty line, (b) Income Support, (c) the poverty trap, (d) net income, (e) the marginal tax rate.
2. What light do the above extracts throw on the causes of poverty in Britain? Can these arguments over the extent of poverty be reconciled?

'If we formulated our ideal of education we might say that we should be taught all that concerns us to know in order that we may become all that concerns us to be.' George Bernard Shaw, *Everybody's Political What's What?*, 1944

The UK government adopted a formal commitment to the provision of education as a result of the passing of the Elementary Education Act in 1870. Prior to that time, education had been available selectively from a wide variety of sources. Private schools sold education on a commercial basis, churches and charitable foundations provided it free, factories offered rudimentary schooling to their child-employees, craftsmen trained apprentices, and some children were taught by their parents. The 1870 Act empowered local Schools Boards (later, local authorities) to provide elementary education generally, to be financed by a combination of fees and government funds. Subsequent Acts made school attendance compulsory for children aged between five and ten years (1880) and then virtually free to all (1891). The 1944 Education Act established the age limits in force today – education free and compulsory between 5 and 15/16 years, free and optional between 16 and 19 years. The 1960s witnessed the expansion of higher education, in the form of colleges of further education and polytechnics. As a result of the Robbins Report of 1963, the university sector was greatly enlarged; free tuition and maintenance grants were available to all students who succeeded in obtaining a university place. Throughout the 1980s, a whole range of schemes were introduced to increase the educational standards of young people who had elected not to stay on at school but who were unsuccessful in obtaining employment – for example, the Youth Training Scheme (YTS) and schemes operated by Training and Enterprise Councils (TECs).

Education as investment
Professor Mark Blaug, who has written much on this topic, has said that the economist who pronounces on the true aims of education exceeds his proper function. So as not to overstep the mark, so to

Let us turn from the physical to the mental state of the workers. Since the bourgeoisie vouch-safes them only so much of life as is absolutely necessary, we need not wonder that it bestows upon them only so much education as lies in the interest of the bourgeoisie; and that, in truth, is not much. The means of education in England are restricted out of all proportion to the population. The few day schools at the command of the working class are available only for the smallest minority, and are bad besides. The teachers, worn-out workers, and other unsuitable persons who only turn to teaching in order to live, are usually without the indispensable elementary knowledge, without the moral discipline so needful for the teacher, and relieved of all public supervision. Here, too, free competition rules, and, as usual, the rich profit by it, and the poor, for whom competition is *not* free, who have not the knowledge needed to enable them to form a correct judgement, have the evil consequences to bear. Compulsory school attendance does not exist. In the mills it is, as we shall see, purely nominal; and when in the session of 1843 the ministry was disposed to make this nominal compulsion effective, the manufacturing bourgeoisie opposed the measure with all its might, thought the working class was outspokenly in favour of compulsory school attendance. Moreover, a mass of children work the whole week through in the mills or at home, and therefore cannot attend school. The evening schools, supposed to be attended by children who are employed during the day, are almost abandoned or attended without benefit. It is asking too much, that young workers who have been using themselves up twelve hours in the day should go to school from eight to ten at night. And those who try it usually fall asleep, as is testified by hundreds of witnesses in the Children's Employment Commission's Report. Sunday schools have been founded, it is true, but they, too, are most scantily supplied with teachers, and can be of use to those only who have already learnt something in the day schools. The interval from one Sunday to the next is too long for an ignorant child to remember in the second sitting what it learned in the first, a week before. The Children's Employment Commission's Report furnishes a hundred proofs, and the Commission itself most emphatically expresses the opinion, that neither the week-day nor the Sunday schools in the least degree meet the needs of the nation. This report gives evidence of ignorance in the working class of England, such as could hardly be expected in Spain or Italy. It cannot be otherwise; the bourgeoisie has little to hope, and much to fear, from the education of the working class.

[From *The Condition of the Working Class in England* by Friedrich Engels (1844)]

speak, we shall define education as the acquisition of new skills and new knowledge. Thus, in reading this book and learning more about the Welfare State, you are presumably undergoing a process of education. If you happen to be enjoying what you read, as you read it, you are receiving **consumption benefits** from education, or pleasure from the process of acquiring knowledge. In addition, you are probably hoping that the book will contain some information of use to you at some later stage of your life – for example, in passing an examination. In this case you are using up your scarce resources in the present (your time) in the expectation of a future gain (an examination pass). In this case, undertaking education clearly yields expected **investment benefits**.

'Investment in oneself' is a central concern of the economics of education, and there are two ways in which the individual might expect this investment of time, resources and effort to pay off. First, individuals who have acquired more skills and more knowledge tend to contribute more to production than do unskilled individuals; i.e. They possess a

---

Of the Education of Costermonger's Children

I have used the heading of 'Education', but perhaps to say 'non-education' would be more suitable. Very few indeed of the costermongers' children are sent even to the Ragged Schools; and if they are, from all I could learn, it is done more that the mother may be saved the trouble of tending them at home, than from any desire that the children shall acquire useful knowledge. Both boys and girls are sent out by their parents in the evening to sell nuts, oranges, & c., at the doors of the theatres, or in any public place, or 'round the houses' (a stated circuit from their place of abode). This trade they pursue eagerly for the sake of 'bunts', though some carry home the money they take, very honestly. The costermongers are kind to their children, 'perhaps in a rough way, and the women make regular pets of them very often.' One experienced man told me, that he had seen a poor costermonger's wife – one of the few who could read – instructing her children in reading; but such instances were very rare. The education of these children is such only as the streets afford; and the streets teach them, for the most part – and in greater or lesser degrees – acuteness – a precocious acuteness – in all that concerns their immediate wants, business, or gratifications; a patient endurance of cold and hunger; a desire to obtain money without working for it; a craving for the excitement of gambling; an inordinate love of amusement; and an irrepressible repugnance to any settled in-door industry.

From *London Labour and the London Poor* by Henry Mayhew (1845)

---

higher marginal product. Firms will pay wages in proportion to workers' marginal products, implying that better educated people can reasonably expect to earn higher incomes.

Figure 11 makes this point in diagrammatic form. The firm, we shall assume, is presently in a competitive market equilibrium. It is setting marginal revenue equal to marginal cost and is maximizing its profits at price P and output Q. Under profit maximization, the firm hires labour at a wage equal to the marginal value of production, or marginal revenue product; that is:

Wage W = product price $P \times$ marginal product MP.

Given diminishing returns to factors of production, marginal product falls as output increases, initially along the line E_1. From the above equation, $P = W/MP$, and the wage at market equilibrium is therefore W_1. Now suppose that the workers undertake an education or training course, which makes them more productive. For each level of output, labour's marginal product is higher; E_1 becomes E_2. As the firm is in competitive equilibrium, it will not wish to alter the product price P or the output Q. However, as the marginal product of labour has risen, then so too will wages, to maintain the identity above. The equilibrium wage for a trained labour force therefore moves to W_2.

Second, the ability to command the higher income depends upon the individual being offered employment to begin with. A record of educational achievement allows the individual to signal his or her abilities to prospective employers, and thus to compete more successfully in the labour market against less qualified individuals. No individual can be certain of obtaining a job, but those better qualified have a better chance of success. Put another way, when selecting amongst job applicants, employers use the applicants' educational records as a way of **screening** out the less able. Thus, for example, an engineering job vacancy may be open only to those with a recognized qualification in engineering. Screening also operates within the education sector itself – universities will only admit students to degree courses if they reach a specified standard in school or college examinations.

Compulsory education

As inferred at the beginning of this chapter, there are essentially two forms of education in the UK. Within a certain age range (approximately 5 to 15 years) it is **compulsory education,** and individuals are legally required to undertake a course of education approved by the state. Outside this age range it is termed **elective education;** i.e. individuals may elect to be educated or trained if they so wish. With slight variations in age range, compulsory and elective education are observable in all industrialized economies. Why is there compulsory education?

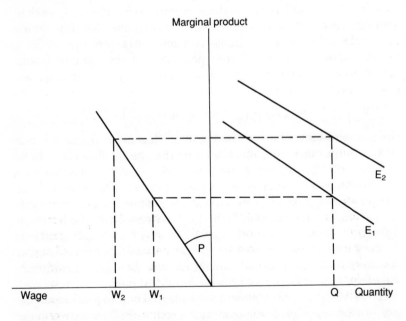

Figure 11 The effect of education on wages

- If individuals were allowed to purchase just as much education as they wished, then they might not purchase enough for their own good. Leaving school at the age of seven years might seem a fine idea at the time, although such a course of action would virtually commit the individual concerned to a life of unemployment and poverty. Not only would this individual fail to realize his full potential, he would represent a constant drain on social security resources. By requiring a minimum period of compulsory education, the government improves individuals' chances in the future. In addition, compulsory education prevents parents from denying educational opportunities to their children.
- As we saw in Chapter 2, education gives rise to external social benefits. Left to their own devices, individuals would not consume enough education for the social good.
- Better educated people are more productive and together create a more powerful and affluent economy. Compulsory education increases the certainty that such an economy will be created (this was the argument which convinced those initially opposing the 1870 Act).

Earlier it was suggested that reading this book was, in itself, an act of education. Curiously enough, if you had borrowed this book from a state school library, your education would have been financed by the public sector. If you had bought it yourself, your education would have been a private market transaction between yourself and the bookshop. More generally, it is evident that tuition in the UK occurs in both state and private schools. Education is clearly a commodity which, in principle, can be provided either publicly or via the market. This having been said, 92 per cent of UK school-children in compulsory education are attending state schools (the proportion is similarly high in other European countries). One obvious reason for this is the unequal distribution of market income which prevails in the UK. If it had to be bought on the market, education would be beyond the reach of the majority of people. Making education compulsory, without providing the resources to purchase it, is simply not feasible.

This argument makes a strong case for government *intervention* in education, but not, it should be stressed, a strong case for government *provision*. From the economic point of view, many of the problems relating to the market provision of education could be resolved in principle by a combination of regulation and subsidy. Consider the following. If all schools were to be operated as private firms, would it be possible to maintain standards? Why not? The hygiene standards of private shops selling food are presently maintained by a **government inspectorate**, so why not the education standards of private schools?

There is, after all, just such an inspectorate presently monitoring standards in state schools. Those private schools currently in operation enter pupils for the same competitive examinations as do the state schools, so presumably they are attempting to achieve the same standards. Indeed, it would actually be irrational for a private school to aim for anything other than the highest obtainable standard, for fear of pupils leaving to attend more successful schools. Without buyers of their 'product' such schools would go out of business. Likewise, public provision is not necessary to enforce participation in education – education could be compulsory without being state-run. All car owners in the UK are obliged to take out insurance policies, although they are at liberty to select whichever private insurance company they care to choose. Applicants for UK passports are obliged to supply a photograph of themselves, but they are not told which photographer to use.

Accepting that the majority of people in the UK would be unable to afford to purchase education were it to be provided by the market, the solution would be to provide such people with the necessary purchasing power and financial support. This could be in the form of increased cash benefits, enabling people to buy as much education as they wished, subject to the statutory minimum. If it were to be felt that people would not buy enough education for the social good, the remedy, as we saw in Chapter 2, would be to subsidize their consumption further. Alternatively, the government might issue **education vouchers** to individuals of school age. These would take the form of a 'pre-paid ticket'. You would take the voucher along to the school of your choice and it would entitle you to enjoy the appropriate period of education. The school would then present the voucher to the government, who would redeem it for cash to cover the school's running costs. One advantage of giving the purchasing power to the consumer would be the requirement for schools to become more competitive and responsive to consumer needs, for fear of losing custom. In fact, both forms of purchasing power transfer are currently in operation in the UK social security system. The government, for example, does not provide free cigarettes or potatoes to the poor; rather, it provides them with money to buy these goods if the families concerned feel they are required. The government also currently issues vouchers of a sort – pensioners are issued tokens for travel on public transport at subsidized prices, for example.

The very existence of private schools attests to the logical possibility of the market provision of compulsory education, accompanied by government regulation and subsidy. The explanation for the dominance of the public sector lies in the fact that, in most countries, the political decision to introduce education rapidly and on a national scale *necessitated* state provision, because of the shortage of private schools and because of the huge scale of investment required. Having established a state system, societies saw no reason to change, especially in view of a number of perceived advantages:

- Cost control is likely to be easier to operate within a centrally organized system. Acting as a monopsonist and by bargaining with teachers nationally, for example, the government may be able to enforce lower wage costs than would be the case were thousands of schools to bargain with their teachers individually.

- As the government possesses complete financial control in a state-provided system, schools are more immediately responsive to government-induced education policy changes. An example is the introduction of the **National Curriculum** in England and Wales in the late 1980s, whereby school syllabuses were proscribed in more detail than before. The maintenance of standards is easier to effect if the government, rather than many different individuals, operates the schools.

- Allowing all schools to become private would possess one distinct economic disadvantage. Local schools and colleges would tend to become local monopolies, by virtue of their close proximity to their pupils. If alternative schools were not easily available to pupils, such schools could raise their fees without losing their customers. They would thus extract an economic rent from the parents who pay the fees. Taxation of the rent would not solve this problem because, with inelastic demand, schools would simply pass on most of the extra costs to parents.

- A common system of state provision creates a less divisive social structure than would a hierarchy of private schools.

Expenditure on compulsory education dominates the government's education budget, and thus contributes to the changing relative budget share which we noted in Figure 6. As we saw, education's share of government expenditure has been in decline in recent years. Two forces have been at work here, pushing in opposite directions. To begin with, real expenditure per pupil has been increasing over time. In fact, it has been growing closely in line with the growth of real GNP, an increase of around 17 per cent between 1971 and 1981, and of around 28 per cent between 1981 and 1989. However, the **demographic profile** of the UK has also been changing quite dramatically. Because local authorities have a legal responsibility to provide school places for each and every child of school age, the amount of money needed for the education budget is a direct function of the number of children of that age. Since the late-1970s, the number of 5- to 16-year-olds in the population has been sharply declining: whilst there were 9.9 million pupils attending primary and secondary schools in 1981, the number had fallen to 8.4 million by 1989. Fewer pupils require fewer schools and fewer teachers. The growth in spending per pupil has thus been offset by a declining number of pupils.

The financing of elective education

Having completed the period of compulsory education, what would induce the individual to train and study further? As was suggested at the beginning of the chapter, further education can be regarded as an investment in oneself, and the educational investment decision which faces school-leavers is modelled in Figure 12. Suppose that two individuals leave school at the same time; one starts work immediately and the other opts to undergo a further period of training. Starting work immediately will provide an annual income of OS_1, gradually rising to OS_1^* by the age of retirement, R years after leaving school. The other person receives further education for E years. This training will necessarily involve him in incurring a cost, OC, each year, in the form of tuition fees, equipment purchase and living expenses. Typically, having received further education, he will then be able to start work at a higher salary than his untrained counterpart (S_2), and the earnings differential

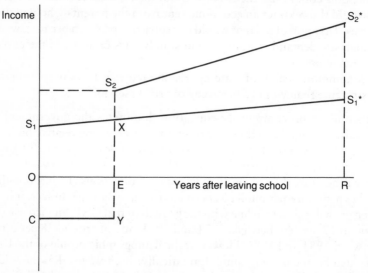

Figure 12 The decision to invest in education

will widen as they both move towards retirement. Which of the two has made the better decision? Clearly, the payoff from further education is the difference between the higher and lower income streams, the area bounded by the points S_2, S_2^*, S_1^* and X. However, in order to obtain this benefit, the more educated individual has had to incur two forms of short-run costs. These are, first, the costs of education (area OEYC) and, second, the income foregone as a result of not starting work immediately after leaving school (area S_1XEO). It therefore follows that education represents a sensible investment of time and resources if the benefits to be expected from education ($S_2S_2^*S_1^*X$) exceed the total costs incurred (S_1XYC). Statistical studies for the UK and for other industrialized economies invariably confirm that each stage of education and training up to and including the university degree level represents a positive investment benefit for the individuals concerned. Long-term gains in net income outweigh short-term costs of education and income foregone.

One central question to be addressed with respect to the above analysis is: where will the individual obtain the resources necessary to finance the short-term costs, prior to the arrival of the long-term benefits? There are a number of possible sources:

- *Self-finance* – The student may undertake training whilst in paid employment, using the latter to subsidize the former.
- *Government* – Tuition remains free in the UK for those electing to remain at school until the age of 19 years, although living expenses have to be met by the student or his family. Students taking certain further education courses, including university degree courses, are eligible for grant assistance.
- *The capital market* – Students might take out a loan from a financial institution, to be paid back out of future earnings.
- *Employers* – Being interested in securing a trained workforce, a firm might pay for training, or even offer it itself.

Figure 13 displays data for eight industrialized countries, relating to the proportion of school-leavers going on to further training during the mid-1980s. The UK appears to be well down the league, especially with respect to full-time education. Several factors account for this. First, the UK government has traditionally played a relatively small role in the provision of further education, with the exception of university education confined to a minority of school-leavers. Second, the capital market for educational finance in the UK has never developed to the same extent as, for example, the **student loans** market in the USA. More

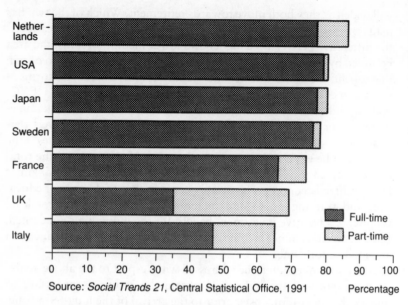

Figure 13 Percentage of 16–18 year olds undergoing further education or training

school-leavers in the USA go on to college than do not, and there exist a great many financial institutions willing and able to offer loan facilities.

Third, a great many labour skills in the past were imparted by private firms under **apprenticeship** schemes. Within such schemes, individuals contracted to work for an employer for a number of years in return for the receipt of training and qualifications. These schemes were regulated by the industries and trades concerned, regulation being necessary to prevent one firm **poaching** the labour of another. The poaching problem is illustrated in Figure 14. Untrained labour, we shall suppose, has a marginal revenue product of MRP_0. The firm will pay labour a wage equivalent to this amount (W_0) but it will also incur costs of training the worker each week during the training period ($T - W_0$). By the end of training it has accordingly made a net outlay equivalent to area A. This it will need to recoup at a later stage, by paying the trained worker a wage (W_1) slightly lower than the worker's higher marginal revenue product (MRP_1) which results from training. In fact, it will set a wage such that area A (training costs) just equals area B (excess of marginal revenue product over wage after training). Clearly, without regulation, it would not pay an enterprise to train labour in such a manner. A rival

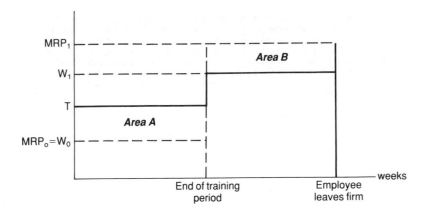

Figure 14 The firm's decision to train labour

firm would simply tempt the employee away after training, by paying a wage equal to the new marginal revenue product, MRP_1. This it could afford to do by virtue of not having incurred training expenses itself, and the original firm would be unable to recoup its costs. The abolition of anti-poaching regulations by the incoming Conservative government of 1979 clearly reduced firms' incentives to train.

In the light of this record, the UK government has, since the mid-1980s, attempted to expand educational opportunities. Under the **Youth Training Scheme**, school-leavers were placed with employers and 'wages' (social security cash benefits) were paid by the government. For certain age-groups, a place on a YTS scheme became a necessary requirement for receiving benefit. In 1991, plans were announced to raise the status of vocational training by introducing new qualifications, and to double the number of students in higher education by the end of the century. This latter objective was to be achieved in part by making economies in the provision of **maintenance grants** for university students. Prior to 1990, students had received a grant from government to meet their living expenses whilst studying. The value of this grant was revised regularly in line with inflation. However, the present system has fixed the money value of the grant, and established a facility whereby students may borrow additional funds, to be paid back at some point in the future. The intention is to bring UK higher education more into line with European practice – the UK government spends four times as much on grants per student as does the French, and ten times as much as does the West German.

After some half-hour's delay, Mr. Squeers reappeared, and the boys took their places and their books, of which latter commodity the average might be about one to eight learners. A few minutes having elapsed, during which Mr. Squeers looked very profound, as if he had a perfect apprehension of what was inside all the books, and could say every word of their contents by heart if he only chose to take the trouble, that gentleman called up the first class.

Obedient to this summons there ranged themselves in front of the schoolmaster's desk, half-a-dozen scarecrows, out at knees and elbows, one of whom placed a torn and filthy book beneath his learned eye.

'This is the first class in English spelling and philosophy, Nickleby,' said Squeers, beckoning Nicholas to stand beside him. 'We'll get up a Latin one, and hand that over to you. Now, then, where's the first boy?'

'Please, sir, he's cleaning the back parlour window,' said the temporary head of the philosophical class.

'So he is, to be sure,' rejoined Squeers. 'We go upon the practical mode of teaching, Nickleby; the regular education system. C-l-e-a-n, clean, verb active, to make bright, to scour. W-i-n, win, d-e-r, der, winder, a casement. When the boy knows this out of book, he goes and does it. It's just the same principle as the use of the globes. Where's the second boy!'

'Please sir, he's weeding the garden,' replied a small voice.

'To be sure,' said Squeers, by no means disconcerted. 'So he is. B-o-t, bot, t-i-n, tin, bottin, n-e-y, ney, bottinney, noun substantive, a knowledge of plants. When he has learned that bottinney means a knowledge of plants, he goes and knows 'em. That's our system, Nickleby; what do you think of it?

[From *The Life and Adventures of Nicholas Nickleby* by Charles Dickens]

Mr Wopsle's great-aunt kept an evening school in the village; that is to say, she was a ridiculous old woman of limited means and unlimited infirmity, who used to go to sleep from six to seven every evening, in the society of youth who paid twopence per week each, for the improving opportunity of seeing her do it. She rented a small cottage, and Mr Wopsle had the room upstairs, where we students used to overhear him reading aloud in a most dignified and terrific manner, and occasionally bumping on the ceiling. There was a fiction that Mr Wopsle 'examined' the scholars, once a quarter. What he did on those occasions was to turn up his cuffs, stick up his hair, and give us Mark Antony's oration over the body of Caesar. This was always followed by Collins's Ode on the Passions, wherein I particularly venerated Mr Wopsle as Revenge, throwing his blood-stained sword in thunder down, and taking the War-denouncing trumpet with a withering look. It was not with me than, as it was in later life, when I fell into the society of the Passions, and compared them with Collins and Wopsle, rather to the disadvantage of both gentlemen. . . .

The Educational scheme or Course established by Mr Wopsle's great-aunt may be resolved into the following synopsis. The pupils ate apples and put straws down one another's backs, until Mr Wopsle's great-aunt collected her energies, and made an indiscriminate totter at them with a birch-rod. After receiving the charge with every mark of derision, the pupils formed in line and buzzingly passed a ragged book from hand to hand. The book had an alphabet in it, some figures and tables, and a little spelling – that is to say, it had had once. As soon as this volume began to circulate, Mr Wopsle's great-aunt fell into a state of coma; arising either from sleep or a rheumatic paroxysm. The pupils then entered among themselves upon a competitive examination on the subject of Boots, with the view of ascertaining who could tread the hardest upon whose toes. This mental exercise lasted until Biddy made a rush at them and distributed three defaced Bibles (shaped as if they had been unskilfully cut off the chump-end of something), more illegibly printed at the best than any curiosities of literature I have since met with, speckled all over with iron mould, and having various specimens of the insect world smashed between their leaves. This part of the Course was usually lightened by several single combats between Biddy and refractory students. When the fights were over, Biddy gave out the number of a page, and then we all read aloud what we could – or what we couldn't – in a frightful chorus; Biddy leading with a high shrill monotonous voice, and none of us having the least notion of, or reverence for, what we were reading about. When this horrible din had lasted a certain time, it mechanically awoke Mr Wopsle's great-aunt, who staggered at a boy fortuitously, and pulled his ears. This was understood to terminate the Course for the evening, and we emerged into the air with shrieks of intellectual victory.

[From *Great Expectations* by Charles Dickens]

KEY WORDS

Consumption benefits	National Curriculum
Investment benefits	Demographic profile
Screening	Student loans
Compulsory education	Apprenticeship
Elective education	Poaching
Government inspectorate	Youth Training Scheme
Education vouchers	Maintenance grants

Reading list

Barr, N., 'Higher education – a suitable case for privatization?', *Economic Review*, Nov. 1989.

Blaug, M., 'The pros and cons of education vouchers', *Economic Review*, May 1987.

Love, J. and Williams, T.D., 'Financing university education: oasis or mirage?', *Royal Bank of Scotland Review*, no. 165, March 1990.

Swann, P. et al., 'Subsidising students', *Economic Review*, Nov. 1988.

Vocational Training, special issue of *National Westminster Bank Quarterly Review*, Feb. 1989.

Wilkinson, M., Chapter 5 in *Equity and Efficiency*, Heinemann Educational, 1992.

Essay topics

1. Critically discuss the possible economic implications of replacing the present system of student grants for higher education with an alternative system such as student loans. (Associated Examining Board, 1990)

2. Explain the difference between consumption and investment. Discuss in which category you would place housing and education. (Joint Matriculation Board, 1987)

3. What benefits does society gain from the provision of state education? Discuss the reasons why some firms are willing to provide finance for the establishment of City Technology Colleges. (Joint Matriculation Board, 1989)

Data Response Question 3

Competition and choice

Read the accompanying extract from the *Independent on Sunday* of 15 September 1991 and answer the following questions.

1. Should students' success in passing examinations be the sole criterion for judging a school's 'performance'? If so, explain why; if not, what other factors would you consider relevant?
2. What 'meaningful information' do you think the government should be supplying to parents?
3. Assuming the proxy market develops fully, how could a school make itself more competitive?
4. Will allowing parents more discretion over choice of schools necessarily lead to their children receiving a better education?

A lesson in the market for schools

. . . Information is crucial if the consumer is to have any real power to discriminate between services, as the teaching profession is beginning to discover. Within the space of a month, three national newspapers have produced comparative tables of schools, two of them concentrating on A-level results. The 1980 and 1988 Education Acts are beginning to work where they were always likely to be most successful. Suddenly the power of information – the power to compare and to criticize – is being put into parents' hands.

Kenneth Baker's 1988 reforms were inspired essentially by economic ideas: competition and choice. In theory, parents are able to choose a school for their child even within the state sector (so long as the school is not up against its baby-boom 1979 admissions limit). The money then follows the pupil, so that parents effectively exercise consumer sovereignty over the education system. To introduce a further element of "supply side flexibility", schools can opt out of local authority control, drawing funds from Whitehall. About a hundred secondary schools out of 4500 have done so, with another hundred in the incubator.

But the essential condition for such a proxy market (where the consumer does not actually pay directly) is the same as for any other market: parents must be able to make informed decisions about the performance of schools. The pressure of opinion – and also ultimately of parents opting to send their children to the better school – will thus gently improve educational standards in exactly the same way as competition improves the standard of washing machines, restaurants and even newspapers. The government, though, is going to have to try harder to present meaningful information.

Chapter Five

Health care

'Health ... is a purchasable commodity, of which a community can possess, within limits, as much or as little as it cares to pay for. It can turn its resources in one direction, and fifty thousand of its members will live who would otherwise have died.' R.H. Tawney, *Equality*, 1931

Health care, as we saw in Table 1, is the only area of the Welfare State where public expenditure has grown consistently over the past two decades. After social security, it is now the biggest item in the UK government's annual expenditure plans. This reflects in part society's belief that health is one of the most important factors in human welfare. Good health enhances the enjoyment of just about every aspect of life, and the value of many other economic benefits – a high income or a good education – are diminished if the individual's health is poor.

It is difficult for people born after the Second World War to appreciate just how revolutionary the formation of the National Health Service (NHS) was. Prior to that time, health care was available free only to a small number of poor individuals accepted for treatment by charitable hospitals. Government involvement was confined to the provision of hospitals catering for infectious diseases. The vast majority of people were therefore required to purchase that health care which they could afford, from individual physicians who operated very much as private firms. The NHS was established on the principle of free access to all citizens, with need rather than income being the criterion for treatment. It was, and continues to be, financed from central government tax revenues, the Consolidated Fund. Until recently, the government has owned and operated most of the hospitals and has employed all the personnel concerned with health care – general practitioners, hospital consultants, nurses, ancillary staff. Over the years, nominal charges have been introduced for certain forms of care, such as drug prescriptions, sight tests and dental care. Even in such cases, charges do not cover costs and patients remain heavily subsidized by the government. A great many patients, moreover, are exempt from such charges.

When they come at last to Tom-all-Alone's, Mr. Bucket stops for a moment at the corner, and takes a lighted bull's-eye from the constable on duty there, who then accompanies him with his own particular bull's-eye at his waist. Between his two conductors, Mr. Snagsby passes along the middle of a villainous street, undrained, unventilated, deep in black mud and corrupt water – though the roads are dry elsewhere – and reeking with such smells and sights that he, who has lived in London all his life, can scarce believe his senses. Branching from this street and its heaps of ruins, are other streets and courts so infamous that Mr. Snagsby sickens in body and mind, and feels as if he were going, every moment deeper down, into the infernal gulf.

"Draw off a bit here, Mr. Snagsby," says Bucket, as a kind of shabby palanquin is borne towards them, surrounded by a noisy crowd. "Here's the fever coming up the street!"

As the unseen wretch goes by, the crowd, leaving that object of attraction, hovers round the three visitors, like a dream of horrible faces, and fades away up alleys and into ruins, and behind walls; and with occasional cries and shrill whistles of warning, thenceforth flits about them until they leave the place.

"Are those the fever-houses, Darby?" Mr. Bucket coolly asks, as he turns his bull's-eye on a line of stinking ruins.

Darby replies that "all them are," and further that in all, for months and months, the people "have been down by dozens," and have been carried out, dead and dying, "like sheep with the rot." Bucket observing to Mr. Snagsby as they go on again, that he looks a little poorly, Mr. Snagsby answers that he feels as if he couldn't breathe the dreadful air.

[From *Bleak House* by Charles Dickens]

The demand for health care

The economics of the NHS are somewhat different from the economics of most other commodities, because of the requirement for health care to be provided free. In consequence, the health care market clears by **quantity adjustment** rather than by **price adjustment**. This may be understood by considering how health care might be provided in a private market – indeed, how it was provided prior to the establishment of the NHS. In Figure 15, the demand for health care, D_1, is downward-sloping; i.e. people demand fewer treatments if the price of treatment rises. Supposing that private hospitals decided to supply A treatments in any one year, then the equilibrium price for medical care would be P_1. If demand were to shift against this chosen supply, from D_1 to D_2,

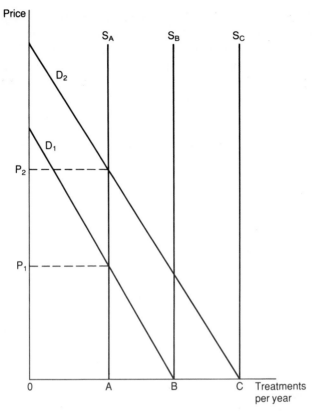

Figure 15 Demand and supply of health care

then the price would change correspondingly, from P_1 to P_2. Under the NHS, however, a market adjustment of this nature does not operate. The NHS supplies health care free of charge (i.e. at a zero price). At such a price, B treatments will be demanded according to demand curve D_1, and the NHS must therefore supply according to the supply curve S_B. The demand rise from D_1 to D_2 in the NHS case cannot be resolved by a price rise as before, because prices are not permitted to rise. In the face of such a rise, *either* more resources would have to be put into health care to raise supply to S_C *or* $(C - B)$ patients would go untreated, and would join the **waiting list** for treatment the following year.

As we saw in the previous chapter, the introduction of compulsory education at the end of the last century allowed a great many people to receive training who, in earlier times, simply could not have afforded it. Similarly, the NHS was intended to offer health care to those who, in the past, had gone without owing to lack of money. It was accordingly anticipated that the first decade of the NHS would require the expenditure of a disproportionate amount of resources as the **backlog of sickness** worked its way through. Demand for health care, it was assumed, would be high initially but would then stabilize over time as the population became more healthy. In consequence, necessary health spending would also stabilize and meet the demand. In fact, these assumptions proved quite mistaken. Increasing demand for health care consistently outstripped the growth of NHS supply, leading to the slow growth of the length of hospital waiting lists.

Why were the founders of the NHS so mistaken about the demand for health care? The answer is that they failed to take account of a number of changes:

- Since the end of the Second World War, the UK has had a progressively **ageing population**. More and more people are surviving into their 70s and beyond, as a result of improved living standards and, ironically enough, better health care. In fact, the proportion of the population aged 65 years and above rose from 13 to 16 per cent between 1971 and 1991. The health needs of the elderly are very much higher than those of the young, simply because the incidence of most illnesses increases with age.

- Prior to the NHS, most people had to accept illness as part of the normal course of events, because they were not in a position to do anything about it. The Welfare State and increasing living standards have created **higher expectations**, implying that ill people nowadays

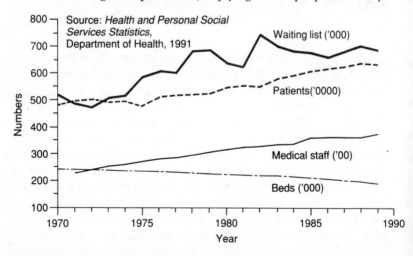

Figure 16 English non-psychiatric hospitals

are much more likely to seek help with their medical problems.

- Advances in **medical technology** have produced treatments and remedies for complaints which, in earlier times, were deemed incurable. In that more and more illnesses can be treated, more and more people are coming forward for treatment.

The increasing number of people on the in-patient waiting lists of English non-psychiatric hospitals is portrayed in Figure 16. Interestingly enough, the data also show that the growth of the waiting list has actually been accompanied by a substantial increase in the number of patients treated each year. Supply of health care has clearly been increasing, but not sufficiently fast to make inroads into the number of cases outstanding. Figure 16 also demonstrates that the capacity of the hospital system – the number of beds available for the treatment of patients – has declined over the past two decades, whilst the number of medical staff has been steadily increasing. The implication is that improvements in medical technology mean that courses of treatment nowadays are concluded in a shorter space of time than before.

Supply: public versus private

When discussing education we noted that, in the UK, the service was provided by both public and private sectors, and there seemed to be nothing intrinsic to education which meant that it *had* to be provided by government. Much the same is true of health care, as is evidenced by the small private health care sector in the UK and, more importantly, by the wide variety of provision systems operating throughout the world. *In fact, the NHS is quite unusual when compared with its counterparts.* Elsewhere in Europe, for example, the most common form of health care supply involves public insurance, very similar in operation to the UK's own National Insurance system of social security benefits. In France and Germany, for example, all employees (and their employers, on their behalf) pay contributions into the public health care insurance fund; some in addition elect to take out private medical insurance. Hospitals are operated both by governments and by the private sector (with government regulation). When a course of treatment is required, the patient chooses the hospital, pays the bills and reclaims most or all of the amount from the insurance funds. Health care in the USA operates in a similar manner for the majority of the population, with the exception that most hospitals and insurance schemes are operated by private entrepreneurs rather than by the government.

We saw earlier that spending on health care in the UK has been growing consistently, yet demand still remains unsatisfied. Does the solution

HOSPITAL WAITING LISTS
The data on the accompanying map display the length of hospital waiting lists for 1990, expressed as a rate per one thousand inhabitants for each of the various Regional Health Authorities of England and Wales. Corresponding data for Scotland and Northern Ireland have also been included. Considerable regional variation is evident – rates in some regions are up to 50 per cent higher than those in others. The rates in all English regions have risen since 1981, with the exception of those in Mersey and the West Midlands, which have fallen. The rate for England as a whole increased from 13.4 to 14.9 per thousand between 1981 and 1990. The rates for Wales and Northern Ireland increased by more than three patients per thousand over the same period, although the rate for Scotland declined (from 13.2 to 11.4).

In 1981, the English waiting list rate was 10.9 per cent of the hospital throughput rate; i.e. for approximately every nine patients treated during that year, one was waiting for treatment. The corresponding figure for 1990 was 9.5 per cent, implying that the rate of increase of hospital throughput was higher than the rate of increase of the waiting lists over the period. A similar pattern can be discerned for Scotland, but the reverse was the case for Wales and Northern Ireland.

In England in 1981, 29.2 per cent of patients had been waiting for treatment for more than 12 months. By the end of the decade the proportion had fallen to 24.0 per cent. The present proportions for Wales and Scotland are lower (21.8 and 12.4 per cent respectively), but that for Northern Ireland is much higher (35.4 per cent).

All these data derive from the Central Statistical Office's *Regional Trends 26* (1991).

to this problem lie in the method of supply? Would the situation be improved if the UK were to adopt one or other of the alternative methods of health care delivery?

Of all the possibilities, the private insurance/private hospital model appears to perform least well when assessed according to efficiency and equity criteria. Under a **private health** insurance system, I would take out medical insurance to avoid having to meet large hospital bills in the event of illness. However, having insured myself against the risk, I have no particular incentive to avoid it, and my insurance premium will pay for as many trips to the doctor as I care to make. Private hospitals will be well aware of this. They will also be aware that the insurance company will meet the bills for my treatment, and they therefore have a strong incentive to push up the price. In response, the insurance company will have to adjust my premium in an attempt to cover its own increasing costs but, as far as I am concerned, higher premiums are still better than the prospect of higher treatment bills. The doctors will get richer and I will get poorer, although the amount of medical care I receive will remain the same.

The US health care system is widely accepted to be prone to this problem – in fact, Americans spend twice as much on health care as do the British, and American doctors are many more times as rich as British ones! Moreover, any insurance system requires that individuals have sufficient income to pay the premiums. Approximately one in five Americans (around 50 million people) receive some assistance with insurance premiums on the grounds of poverty and/or old-age, although a further 40 million receive no assistance yet are too poor to be able to afford any medical insurance. Finally, the US medical system is extremely bureaucratic, in view of all the invoicing and reimbursements which have to take place. Administration costs have been estimated at 20 per cent of total revenue; by comparison, the cost of NHS administration amounts to just over 5 per cent of total health care spending.

Public insurance systems have slightly more to commend them on equity grounds, because the contributions system can be geared into social security and complete coverage can thereby be ensured. As the central government has direct control over payouts, it is also in a better position to monitor cost increases and to prevent the extraction of extra profits on the part of private, profit-maximizing hospitals. Administrative costs, nevertheless, tend to be higher than under the NHS model, again because of the need to invoice each and every treatment.

Over the past few decades, health care costs have risen dramatically in all industrialized countries, although the rises have been very much lower in the NHS owing to the highly centralized system of organization. As the employer of health care personnel and the operator of hospitals, the government has been in a strong position to prevent health care cost inflation, to which the US system in particular has proved especially prone. However, just because the NHS has proved cheaper than other national systems does not mean it has necessarily been perfectly effective. Scope for improvement might well exist. Following this line of argument, a series of NHS reforms was announced in 1989, entailing the creation of an internal market.

The internal market

Under the pre-reform NHS system, an individual would approach his general practitioner (GP), either for treatment or for referral to a hospital. At no stage of the process would money change hands, as it were, because every aspect of patient care would be financed from central government. This lack of a market structure was felt to pose a number of efficiency problems:

- Patients were obliged to register with their local GP. As he faced no competition from other GPs, he had no particular incentive to offer a high quality of service.
- GPs referred patients to their local district hospital. As this hospital faced no competition for patients from hospitals outside the district it had no particular incentive to ensure that its production of treatments was at as low a cost as possible, or that its quality of service was high. Most importantly, it had no incentive to reduce its waiting list.
- As the costs of drugs were met by central government (and, to a lesser extent, by patients themselves), GPs faced no incentive to limit drug prescribing.
- GPs faced no incentives to engage in **preventive medicine**.
- Doctors were unable to use the resources of the private health care sector for their NHS patients.

Under the **internal market** system, patients will be able to register with the GP of their choice. **GP budgets** will be provided from the government's Consolidated Fund, the size of the budget depending on the number of patients who register with the GP and the extent of the medical needs of those patients. GPs will establish treatment contracts with whichever hospital (public or private) they care to chose. When a patient is referred to the hospital, the GP will purchase the treatment from his budget on the patient's behalf. This purchase price represents the source of revenue for the hospital. In the long run, it is intended that the majority of hospitals will become **NHS Hospital Trusts.** Unlike pre-reform hospitals, Trusts will have considerable managerial and financial autonomy. They will, for example, be able to hire and fire staff, negotiate their own wage agreements, choose which courses of treatment they are prepared to offer, and use their profits for service development. GPs will also be set drug prescribing budgets and targets for preventive medicine (e.g. cancer screening, health promotion clinics and immunization).

The internal market is intended to remedy the incentive problems mentioned above. GPs will now be obliged to compete for patients, and those offering unsatisfactory service will find their patients (and thus part of their budget) transferring to GPs elsewhere. Meeting preventive medicine targets will bring financial rewards, and savings on the budget may be used for the development of the practice. Hospitals (both public and private) will be obliged to compete for revenue from GPs, requiring them to monitor their costs closely and to deliver a high quality of service.

Two sets of problems may be anticipated with respect to this move towards the internal market, and the first of these are the problems of transition. To begin with, GPs and hospitals have had, in the past, very little experience of buying and selling and these are principles which will have to be learned. As the system is being phased in gradually over the next few years, there is good reason to believe that, in the short term, patients of budget-holding GPs will receive better treatment at the expense of those of non-budget holding GPs, because all hospitals will be anxious to gain a foothold in the developing market. This, in turn, has given rise to a certain amount of public concern.

Over the longer term, a number of the problems of transition ought to be overcome in some degree. Hospitals, one would predict, will become more adept and experienced at setting their prices and controlling their costs. As a progressively higher proportion of GPs become responsible for their own budgets, the discrimination of the 'two-tier' system should disappear. Given that the transition is unlikely to be completed for a number of years, only tentative forecasts of future, long-term operations can be made. **Efficiency gains** may well be realized as hospitals become more competitive, although these gains could easily be counter-balanced by the increased administrative costs of invoicing and recording. We have already observed the predictable trend of the amalgamation of GPs into larger group practices, which reap **economies of scale.** Instances have also been recorded of GPs refusing to admit some patients to their practices, on the grounds that such patients would demand a disproportionate amount of care and erode the GP's budget.

Patients pay price of the market

The government's new "health market" in the NHS is running into serious difficulties only weeks after it was introduced – and patients are paying the price. As the so-called market grinds into action major problems are emerging:

- Huge variations in the price of different operations, prompting health authorities to choose the cheapest rather than the best. This could lead to the closure of a major teaching hospital in London.
- A two-tier system of health care, with budget-holding GPs with large practices carving out for themselves and their patients a better deal at the expense of non-fund-holding colleagues.
- Restriction of patient choice, with people being told they cannot go to the hospital they want because the health authority does not have a contract with it. . . .

The impact of market forces is felt most strongly in the capital. Prices at the prestigious London teaching hospitals are proving to be 50 per cent higher than those of outer London and the Home Counties. The cost of having an ovary removed, for example, is £2299 at Guy's Hospital, London, £1630 at St Bartholomew's but only £918 at King George's Hospital, Ilford, Essex. The variations in price explain why Guy's Hospital is having to shed 600 jobs in order to become more competitive and attract more work. . . .

The scandal of the emergent two-tier system is typified in Leeds and Watford, where fund-holding GPs have won agreements from local hospitals that their patients will be treated within three months. But patients from non-fund-holding practices – which account for 90 per cent – will have to wait just as long as before, and perhaps even longer, because others have "jumped the queue". . . .

Dr Brian Lewis, consultant anaesthetist at the William Harvey Hospital in Ashford, Kent, and a member of the BMA's Council, said: "The Health Services Act lays a duty on the Secretary of State for Health to provide for the diagnosis, treatment and prevention of disease. At the moment the government has not got a proper plan. They claim that a market will make us nicer to our patients. That makes about as much sense as telling a wartime fishmonger that he has to be nice to his customers, when he only has enough fish for about half the queue. In times of shortages, as there is for health care, the customer does not have a chance to go elsewhere. People are queuing up to get into my hospital. I am nice to my patients anyway. But if I weren't, the market wouldn't make me."

Source: *Observer*, 5 May 1991

Meeting health needs

The 1979 Royal Commission on the NHS reflected that it had no difficulty in believing one expert witness who suggested that the UK could quite easily spend its entire GNP on health care. All economies are finding that, whatever their current level of health spending, needs remain unmet and, indeed, it is not difficult to point to areas where more *could* be spent – on hospitals to reduce the waiting lists, on medical research to develop solutions to presently incurable illnesses, on more sophisticated aids and appliances for the handicapped and disabled, on mass screening programmes for preventable disease. Given that resourcing will inevitably fall short of needs, it is important for a **rationing** criterion to be established, to ensure the best use of limited health care resources.

This use of the word 'best' requires the specification of an outcome measure for health care. Amongst those commonly used are reductions in mortality or increases in survival rates following a course of treatment. Thus if might be said that, if we have to choose between two alternative uses of health care resources, we should devote those resources to the treatment which produces, for example, the greatest mortality reduction. Recently, health economists have been advocating the use of the **quality-adjusted life-year**, or QALY, as the most appropriate outcome measure. A quality-of-life index has been constructed, based upon patient distress and disability, which assigns the value 1 to normal health. The poorer the patient's health, the lower his score on the index. One QALY is thus one year of life at normal health or any one of a number of combinations of years of life and quality of life; for example, 4 years with a 0.2 score, or 10 years with a 0.1 score.

The manner in which QALYs are identified is illustrated in Figure 17. Suppose a patient arrives at hospital with a particular disease and a quality-of-life score of 0.5. The prognosis suggests a steady deterioration in health status and death in three years, a quality-of-life path represented by line A in Figure 17. However, treatment can be expected to return him to close to perfect health within one year (an index value of 0.9), and provide an additional life expectancy of ten

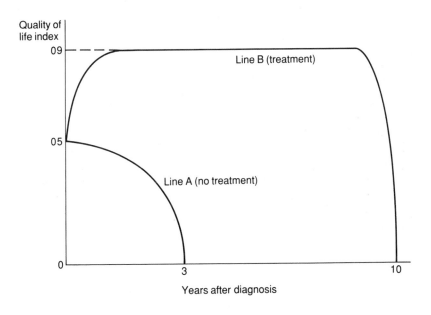

Figure 17 The QALY gains from treatment

years. This quality-of-life path is represented by line B. The number of QALYs resulting from the treatment is therefore given by the area between lines A and B. Knowing the total cost of the treatment, it is therefore possible to calculate a 'cost per QALY gained'.

Economists have already estimated such costs per QALY for a number of treatments, and more are being worked out all the time. Hip replacement, for example, has been costed at £750 per QALY gained, and operations on brain tumours at £70 000. The implications for resource allocation now become evident. Spending £1 million on these alternatives would yield either 14 QALYs from brain tumour operations or 1333 QALYs from hip replacements. It is thus far more effective to spend the money on the latter at the expense of the former. Clearly, all treatments could be ranked in terms of their costs per QALY gained, and treatments offering low costs would take precedence over those offering high costs.

Using QALYs as a rationing device to decide just who to treat poses the ethical question of who shall receive priority in treatment. However, it is important to remember that, *as long as resources are scarce relative to needs, some form of rationing – entailing an ethical choice – is inevitable.* The QALY criterion is simply one amongst many. Perhaps you might personally prefer rationing at random, or 'first come, first served'. Even price-adjustment health care systems, such as that of the USA, rest on ethical judgements about rationing – specifically, that it is fair that health care goes to those who can afford to pay.

Washing among chimney-sweepers seems to be much more frequent than it was. In the evidence before parliament it was stated that some of the climbing-boys were washed once in six months, some once a week, some once in two or three months. I do not find it anywhere stated that any of these children were never washed at all; but from the tenour of the evidence it may be reasonably concluded that such was the case.

A master sweeper, who was in the habit of bathing at the Marylebone baths once and sometimes twice a week, assured me that, although many now eat and drink and sleep sooty, washing is more common among his class than when he himself was a climbing-boy. He used then to be stripped, and compelled to step into a tub, and into water sometimes too hot and sometimes too cold, while his mistress, to use his own word, *scoured* him. Judging from what he had seen and heard, my informant was satisfied that, from 30 to 40 years ago, climbing-boys, with a very few exceptions, were but seldom washed; and then it was looked upon by them as a most disagreeable operation, often, indeed, as a species of punishment. Some of the climbing-boys used to be taken by their masters to bathe in the Serpentine many years ago; but one boy was unfortunately drowned, so that the children could hardly be coerced to go into the water afterwards.

[From *London Labour and the London Poor* by Henry Mayhew (1845)]

KEY WORDS

Quantity adjustment
Price adjustment
Waiting list
Backlog of sickness
Ageing population
Higher expectations
Medical technology
Health insurance

Preventive medicine
Internal market
GP budgets
NHS Hospital Trusts
Efficiency gains
Economies of scale
Rationing
Quality-adjusted life-year

Reading list

Chalkley, M., 'Costs and NHS reforms', *Economic Review*, Nov. 1991.

Cullis, J. and Jones, P., 'Economics of NHS waiting lists', *Economic Review*, May 1988.

Health Care Survey, supplement to *The Economist*, 6 July 1991.

Whynes, D., 'Economic perspectives on the National Health reforms', Economics Association, autumn 1991.

Wilkinson, M., Chapter 5 in *Equity and Efficiency*, Heinemann Educational, 1992.

Essay topics

1. Assess the economic arguments for and against providing a health service free of charge to everyone in the community. (Associated Examining Board, 1988)
2. Discuss the economic arguments for and against the imposition of high taxes to deter cigarette smoking. (Associated Examining Board, 1987)
3. Define what is meant by (a) a merit good, and (b) externalities. Discuss the relevance of these concepts to the subject of health care. (University of London School Examinations Board, 1991)
4. 'The creation of an internal market in the National Health Service will increase the choice, cut waiting times and improve the quality of the service provided' (Rt Hon Kenneth Clarke, MP). Discuss. (Oxford and Cambridge Schools Examination Board, 1991)

Data Response Question 4

Health and economic status

Read the accompanying extract from the *Guardian* of 12 June 1991 and answer the following questions.

1. Distinguish between *relative* and *absolute* income.
2. Why would you expect health to be 'intimately related to social and economic status'?
3. Why might unemployment be 'bad for health'?
4. Not only are Americans twice as rich as Greeks or Spaniards, but they spend twice the proportion of their national product on health care (6 per cent compared with 12 per cent). Are Americans therefore wasting their money?
5. Do you agree that 'tackling the links between poverty and health' is not a 'realistic objective' of government policy?

Inequality is bad for your health

According to Health Secretary William Waldegrave, tackling the links between poverty and health is a "perfectly legitimate" though not realistic objective for government policy. The issues involved were too fundamental, too complicated and too enduring for the reduction of health inequalities to be included among the government's health policy targets.

If this was once a plausible view, the striking picture emerging from recent research means that it no longer is. It appears that the degree of economic inequality in society not only affects the scale of its health inequalities, but also provides the most important key we know of to the improvement of the health of a nation as a whole. It has always been clear that health is intimately related to social and economic status. But while we might have expected the link to weaken as we got richer, it has been getting stronger: bigger class differences are found in more diseases.

Research suggests that the death rates of the least well-off in our society do respond, as you would expect, to changes in their incomes. Moreover, there is good evidence that forms of deprivation like unemployment are bad for health. However, there is a puzzle here. If health is related to income and the standard of living *within* Britain and other countries, surely it should also be related to the differences in the standard of living between countries. But it is not. Comparisons among the affluent countries show that life expectancy is little affected by differences in either their living standards or their rates of economic growth.

The answer to this paradox is that, once countries have reached the standards of affluence of the developed world, further increases in *absolute* income cease to matter very much. Thus, the UK, Luxemburg and (what was) West Germany are twice as rich per capita and yet have lower life expectancies than Greece or Spain. It turns out that what matters in rich countries is *relative* income, that is to say, the scale of income differences within countries. During the 1980s income distribution widened particularly dramatically in Britain and is now the widest since good records began. In his report *On The State Of The Public Health In 1989*, the Chief Medical Officer at the Department of Health pointed out that death rates for British men and women throughout the 15–45 age range had actually been rising each year since 1985 – a trend which he said was not the result of Aids deaths.

As well as explaining why health is related to income differences within, but not between, developed countries, income inequality also explains why class differences in death rates have not diminished in the post-war period – despite the unparalleled rise in prosperity. If health inequalities were a reflection of absolute deprivation, then rising post-war affluence would surely have reduced the proportion of the population affected. That this has not happened indicates the crucial role of relative, over absolute, income.

R.G. Wilkinson

Chapter Six
Housing

'In general, there is not perhaps any one article of expense or consumption by which the liberality or narrowness of a man's whole expense can be better judged of than by his house-rent.' Adam Smith, *Wealth of Nations*, 1776

In 1914, nine out of ten households lived in accommodation rented from private landlords, and only one out of ten lived in properties which they themselves owned. Since that time, the picture has changed dramatically. Nowadays:

- two-thirds of all UK dwellings are **owner-occupied** – i.e. inhabited by people who either own the property outright or who are buying it with the aid of a loan from a financial institution such as a building society;
- one-quarter of all dwellings are owned and rented out to families by local authorities;
- fewer than one-in-ten dwellings are owned and rented out by private landlords.

The twentieth century in the UK has therefore seen substantial expansions of the owner-occupied and **public rental** housing sectors, at the expense of the **private rental** sector. Figure 18 displays the trends in the stock of housing in Great Britain over the past two decades. These data confirm the continued expansion of the owner-occupied sector and the contraction of the supply of private rental accommodation. The public sector housing stock, it should be noted, peaked in the late-1970s and has since gradually declined.

Adequate shelter is one of the most fundamental of human wants, and government intervention in the housing market has a long history. Government involvement at a national level began in the nineteenth century, largely out of a concern for public health. Authority was granted to local government to demolish unsafe or unhealthy homes, and to ensure minimum building standards for new ones. Because building to a standard is more expensive than building in the absence of standards, construction costs rose, and the effect of

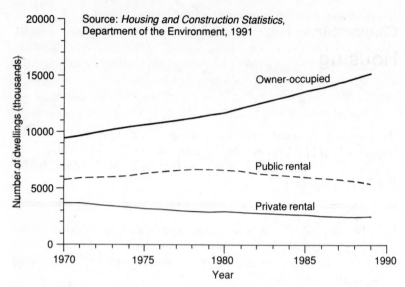

Figure 18 Great Britain's housing stock

both of these measures was to reduce the supply of rented accommodation, the principal form of housing at the time. Accordingly, the market price for accommodation rose and many people found they could no longer afford the rents. During and after the First World War, two policy measures were enacted – **rent control** in the private sector and a programme of local authority house-building.

Let us investigate some of the slums in their order. London comes first, and in London the famous rookery of St Giles which is now, at last, about to be penetrated by a couple of broad streets. St Giles is in the midst of the most populous part of the town, surrounded by broad, splendid avenues in which the gay world of London idles about, in the immediate neighbourhood of Oxford Street, Regent Street, of Trafalgar Square and the Strand. It is a disorderly collection of tall, three of four-storied houses, with narrow, crooked, filthy streets, in which there is quite as much life as in the great thoroughfares of the town, except that, here, people of the working class only are to be seen. A vegetable market is held in the street, baskets with vegetables and fruits, naturally all bad and hardly fit to use, obstruct the sidewalk still further, and from these, as well as from the fish-dealers' stalls, arises a horrible smell. The houses are occupied from cellar to garret, filthy within and without, and their appearance is such that no human being could possibly wish to live in them. But all this is nothing in comparison with the dwellings in the narrow courts and alleys between the streets, entered by covered passages between the houses, in which the filth and tottering ruin surpass all description. Scarcely a whole window-pane can be found, the walls are crumbling, door-posts and window-frames loose and broken, doors of old boards nailed together, or altogether wanting in this thieves' quarter, where no doors are needed, there being nothing to steal. Heaps of garbage and ashes lie in all directions, and the foul liquids emptied before the doors gather in stinking pools. Here live the poorest of the poor, the worst paid workers with thieves and the victims of prostitution indiscriminately huddled together, the majority Irish, or of Irish extraction, and those who have not yet sunk in the whirlpool of moral ruin which surrounds them, sinking daily deeper, losing daily more and more of their power to resist the demoralizing influence of want, filth, and evil surroundings.

[From *The Condition of the Working Class in England* by Friedrich Engels (1844)]

The private rental market

The imposition of ceilings on rents, combined with regulations relating to housing standards and security of tenure, has been an ingredient of UK housing policy since 1915. It has, moreover, been seen as the principal cause of the decline in the UK private rental sector since that time. Using simple economic analysis, it is not difficult to understand why. Rent control is intended to address the problem of family poverty caused by the unavoidable requirement of having to meet rent bills. Left to the market, it has been argued, rents would be so high that many families would either face eviction or would have hardly any disposable income left after the deduction of housing expenses.

Figure 19 illustrates the effects of imposing rent control. Let us initially suppose that the housing rental market is in equilibrium. With the given housing demand and supply, Q_e units of housing are being consumed at a rent, or price, of P_e per unit. The government now assesses this rent as being too high for the average tenant and enforces a price ceiling of P_c. Three conclusions may immediately be drawn:

- At this lower price, property letting becomes less attractive to landlords and the supply of accommodation accordingly contracts along the supply curve. With lower returns from renting out accomodation, some landlords would wish to realize their assets by selling off their properties to owner-occupiers or to property-developers. The

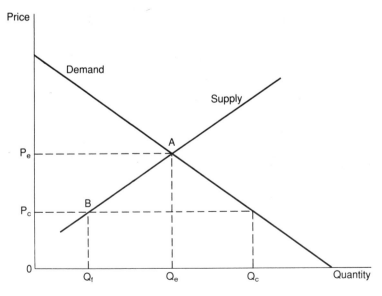

Figure 19 The effect of rent control

money thus raised could then be invested in economic activities more profitable than house rental. At the ceiling price in Figure 19, landlords are only willing to offer Q_f units of housing; i.e. the stock of accommodation available for rent falls by $(Q_e - Q_f)$ units.

- The total rent income received by landlords falls, from P_eAQ_eO to P_cBQ_fO. A portion of this loss incurred by landlords represents, of course, the rent saved $(P_e - P_c)$ by each of those tenants who remain in rented accommodation. Thus rent control effects a transfer from landlords to tenants. However, with less revenue coming in to cover costs, some landlords might attempt to economize on the routine maintenance of their properties. Indeed, it has been estimated that around 40 per cent of all sub-standard dwellings are in the private rental sector, although this sector comprises less than 10 per cent of all dwellings.
- At this lower, controlled price, there is an excess demand for accommodation, of an amount $(Q_c - Q_f)$. Households attracted into the rental market by the prospect of paying lower rents will find their accommodation needs unmet.

The imposition of rent controls, it may be concluded, is likely to contract both the quantity and the quality of the accommodation available. In addition, certain other objections to the practice may be noted:

- A tenant living in rent-controlled housing may feel that, were he to move to a new area, he would be unlikely to obtain such cheap accommodation. Other things remaining equal, this could deter him from moving; i.e. rent controls may contribute to **labour immobility**.
- Rent control and security of tenure benefits those who already inhabit controlled accommodation, at the expense of those who do not. To some extent, it is the most needy who find it hardest to obtain such accommodation. With security of tenure and protection from eviction, landlords will prefer to let their properties to those who they consider offer least risk of rent default or damage (e.g. individuals in full-time employment as opposed to large families dependent on social security).
- The redistributive effects of rent control are arbitrary – not all landlords are rich and not all tenants are poor. In some cases, therefore, a poor landlord may be effectively subsidizing a rich tenant, which runs counter to the normal philosophy of redistribution.

Although the tenants concerned clearly benefit individually from the subsidies which they receive as a result of rent control, the mechanism overall appears to suffer from substantial defects. In consequence, a series of Housing Acts in the 1980s has been aimed at overturning the structure of rent controls established since the beginning of the century. The growth of an uncontrolled private rental sector, for example, has been encouraged. Those rents remaining controlled are now set with as much a view towards guaranteeing a fair return for landlords as to ensuring a fair price for tenants.

The long-term intention is to return the allocation of private rented accommodation to the operation of market forces. Naturally, the abolition of rent control will entail a rise in rents, as might be anticipated from Figure 19. The intention, however, is to use housing benefit (discussed in Chapter 3) to augment the income of the poorer families, so that they can afford to pay the higher rents. From the tenant's point of view (Figure 19), it clearly makes no difference whether (i) he pays rent P_c for his accommodation or (ii) he pays rent P_e and receives housing benefit ($P_e - P_c$). However, the use of housing benefit to assist in meeting the accommodation needs of the poor means that it is now the government, and not the landlord, who is paying the subsidy. In theory, the aforementioned problems of rent control should now be overcome. Landlords receiving the market rent have no incentive to reduce quality or quantity. Labour mobility is not reduced, as benefits are attached to persons rather than to property. Housing Benefit is targeted towards the poor and, as a result, only those who need assistance will receive it.

Local authority housing

Subsidizing rents, it seems, gives rise to adverse supply effects when left to the market. Local authority housing attempts to side-step these negative effects of rent control by combining rent subsidies with the direct public provision of housing. The long-term local authority building programme was initiated by the 1919 Housing Act and, by 1930, 7 per cent of all dwellings were publicly owned. This proportion gradually increased over time and reached around 32 per cent in the late-1970s. Since that time, the public sector share has fallen (Figure 18).

The principal reasons for this reversal in the fortunes of public sector housing over the past two decades are the following:

- The two Conservative governments of the period (1970–74 and 1979 to date) have typically been less well-disposed than the Labour government (1974–79) towards the public sector's role in the provision of new housing. The former's policy orientation has been more towards creating the conditions for the extension of the private sector. Figure 20 charts year-by-year additions to the housing stock and, as may be seen, the only significant upturn in public sector house-building occurred in the mid-1970s.

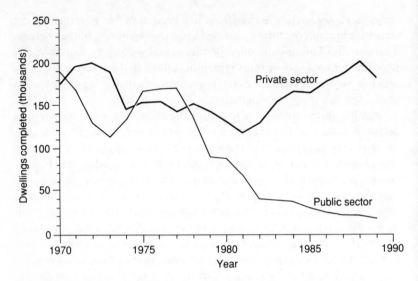

Figure 20 New dwellings completed each year

- Even if local authorities had been well disposed towards house-building in the 1980s, they were suffering severe financial problems which limited their capacity to undertake major investment projects. Over one-half of all local authority spending is financed by grants from central government, and the value of these grants was gradually being reduced. In addition, the government introduced **rate-capping** (later, 'community-charge capping'), whereby local authorities attempting to raise local revenues by an amount deemed excessive by central government were penalized by a corresponding loss of central government grant.
- The 1980 Housing Act incorporated a "Right to Buy" policy, which entitled local authority tenants to purchase their houses at subsidized prices. The extent of the subsidy depended on the length of tenancy, the longest-standing tenants being eligible for discounts of 50 per cent. Within a few years, over one million houses were thus transferred from local authorities to the owner-occupied sector.

Public sector housing generates many of the same economic problems already identified in the case of private rental accommodation. Rents have tended to be set at below-market rates in an attempt to improve tenants' living standards, and this has created excess demand analogous to that found in the private rental sector. Again, rent subsidies immobilize labour but do not necessarily ensure that it is only the poor who receive the subsidy benefit.

Owner-occupied housing

We have seen that government intervenes in the private rental market
by means of regulation (rent control) and in the public rental market by
direct provision and subsidy. Intervention in the private owner-occupied sector takes the form of **tax expenditure**. Tax expenditure is not
direct spending *per se*; instead, it is implicit spending by virtue of the
government electing not to levy as much tax as it otherwise might.

The majority of households buying their own homes are doing so on
the basis of a long-term loan or mortgage from a financial institution.
The interest payments on such a loan are tax-deductible. They are, in
other words, subject to **tax relief**, by being added to other allowances to
determine the level of the household's tax threshold. The government is
thus choosing not to tax that part of household income allocated to
repaying loans on house purchase. In fact, by the late-1980s, tax expenditure on private house purchase amounted to approximately
£5 billion, slightly more than total public spending on housing (exclud-
ing housing benefit).

The effect of making interest payments tax-deductible is to raise the
disposable income of the household, and therefore to make it easier for
people to buy their own homes. Figure 21 illustrates the point. Without
tax-deductibility, a household would pay no tax until reaching the tax
threshold, T, and it would then pay tax at the prevailing marginal rate.
Thus a pre-tax income of Y would yield a post-tax or disposable
income of A, from which loan repayments would have to be made.

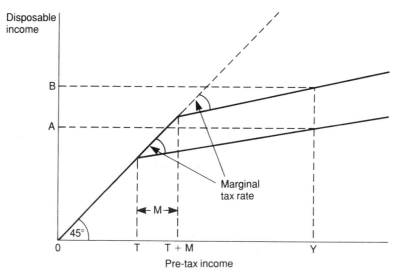

Figure 21 The effect of mortgage tax relief

With tax-deductibility, however, the household's mortgage interest payments, M, raise its tax threshold to T + M, and the household pays tax at the same marginal rate above this level as before. A pre-tax income of Y thus yields a higher disposable income, B, from which the same loan repayments would have to be made.

As Figure 18 demonstrated, owner-occupation is the largest of the housing sectors and has had the fastest growth in recent years. This growth is not, however, being accomplished without difficulties, owing to rising and falling house prices and the impact of the late-1980s economic recession. The accompanying extract from the *Guardian* ('Record number of homes lost') relates to the repossession of homes by financial institutions from households unable to meet the repayments – for comparison, there were approximately 3000 repossessions in 1980.

Record number of homes lost

Record numbers of homes were repossessed in the first half of this year, because of the deepening recession and its toll on jobs. There has also been a dramatic rise in the number of home-buyers who have fallen behind with their mortgage payments. Figures released yesterday by the Council of Mortgage Lenders (CML) show that a record 36,610 homes were repossessed. This is more than a third higher than the number repossessed in the second half of last year, and double the figure for the same period last year. In the whole of last year 43,890 homes were repossessed.

The number of homebuyers 6 to 12 months behind on their mortgage payments also rose by almost a third, to 162,210, the highest level recorded; and there was a jump of more than 65 per cent, to 59,690, in the number more than 12 months in arrears. This means that one in 44 homebuyers is now at least six months behind.

The overall picture is worse, as figures on those less than six months in arrears are not included.

Mark Boleat, the director general of CML, said the "disappointing" figures were further evidence of recession. Job losses and insecurity are having greater impact on home buyers than during previous periods of high unemployment; partly because of the number of low-income families who bought council homes, but also because this recession is hitting people in the South East who took out large mortgages when the market was high. . . . Mr Boleat believes the rise in the number of homebuyers 12 months in arrears reflects increasing efforts by lenders to reschedule debts so people can stay put. Others feel lenders are less inclined to repossess as it is difficult to sell.

Source: Adapted from the *Guardian*, 16 August 1991

The excess demand for housing

That excess demand for satisfactory housing in the UK generally exists can be seen from a variety of sources of evidence:

- The rationing of local authority housing takes place in much the same way as the rationing of health care under the pre-reform NHS; i.e. the names of applicants are added to a waiting list. The present waiting list for local authority accommodation is in excess of 1.5 million applicants long.

- By law, local authorities are obliged to provide accommodation for certain classes of household who declare themselves to be homeless. Households which meet the criteria of priority need will be housed in local authority accommodation, if available, or in private sector accommodation rented by the local authority. Amongst the more important **priority need** criteria are the existence of children in the household, pregnancy, old age, and homelessness as a result of a natural disaster. Approximately 150 000 priority need families are offered accommodation each year.

- Survey evidence reveals that approximately one in ten housholds in the UK are either living in overcrowded conditions, *or* are sharing accommodation unwillingly, *or* are living in accommodation lacking basic amenities or requiring major repairs.

- The number of truly homeless people in the UK – that is, individuals with no place of residence and who have 'taken to the streets' – is unknown, although surveys have estimated the number as being not less than 200 000 at any one time. The majority are to be found in the big cities, such as London, Birmingham and Glasgow. Contrary to the popular belief, the homeless do not comprise solely elderly tramps and alcoholics. They are far more likely to be unemployed men and women in their late-teens and early-twenties, who have left home owing to family disputes or family poverty.

Jo lives – that is to say, Jo has not yet died – in a ruinous place, known to the like of him by the name of Tom-all-Alone's. It is a black, dilapidated street, avoided by all decent people; where the crazy houses were seized upon, when their decay was far advanced, by some bold vagrants, who, after establishing their own possession, took to letting them out in lodgings. Now, these tumbling tenements contain, by night, a swarm of misery. As, on the ruined human wretch, vermin parasites appear, so these ruined shelters have bred a crowd of foul existence that crawls in and out of gaps in walls and boards; and coils itself to sleep, in maggot numbers, where the rain drips in; and comes and goes, fetching and carrying fever, and sowing more evil in its every footprint than Lord Coodle, and Sir Thomas Doodle, and the Duke of Foodle, and all the fine gentlemen in office, down to Zoodle, shall set right in five hundred years – though born expressly to do it.. . .

Jo comes out of Tom-all-Alone's meeting the tardy morning which is always late in getting down there, and munches his dirty bit of bread as he comes along. His way lying through many streets, and the houses not yet being open, he sits down to breakfast on the door-step of the Society for the Propagation of the Gospel in Foreign Parts, and gives it a brush when he has finished, as an acknowledgement of the accommodation. He admires the size of the edifice, and wonders what it's all about. He has no idea, poor wretch, of the spiritual destitution of a coral reef in the Pacific, or what it costs to look up the precious souls among the cocoa-nuts and bread-fruit.

[From *Bleak House* by Charles Dickens]

KEY WORDS

Owner-occupied	Rate-capping
Public rental	Tax expenditure
Private rental	Tax relief
Rent control	Priority need
Labour immobility	

Reading list

Hurl, B., Chapter 2 in *Privatization and the Public Sector*, 2nd edn, Heinemann Educational, 1992.

Johnson, P., 'Measuring poverty', *Economic Review*, Nov. 1990.

Paisley, R and Quillfeldt, J., Chapter 1 (The housing market) in *Economics Investigated*, Collins Educational, 1989.

Essay topics

1. Outline the case for and against (a) public sector provision of housing, (b) other forms of intervention in the housing market. (University of Oxford Delegacy of Local Examinations, 1990)
2. To what extent do supply and demand determine the provision of housing, health care and teachers? (University of London School Examinations Board, 1990)
3. As Chancellor of the Exchequer, Nigel Lawson said that 'the business of government should never be the government of business'. Do you agree with him? (University of Cambridge Local Examinations Syndicate, 1989)

Data Response Question 5

The UK housing market

This task is based on an examination question set by the Oxford and Cambridge Schools Examination Board in 1989. Read the article, which is adapted from the *Daily Telegraph* in late 1988, and answer the questions.

1. Why are increases in interest rates likely to moderate the rise in house prices?
2. Why might it be the case that the RPI plays down the impact of rising house prices?

3. What factors *other than those mentioned above* might account for the rapid escalation of house prices?
4. How does house price inflation feed through the rest of the economy?
5. Why does the article conclude that 'those with large mortgages will feel the pinch'?

Soaring house prices have become the test of the government's commitment to controlling inflation, with the latest rise in the mortgage rate seen as the first stage in a determined campaign to take the heat out of the housing market. *If house prices do not slow in the autumn, interest rates are likely to be progressively increased, until they eventually do.* The country is in the grip of a housing boom the like of which has not been seen since the mid-1970s. The average house now costs 28 per cent more than a year ago and 55 per cent more in East Anglia. For many people already well established on the housing ladder, appreciating property values are a source of comfort, making them feel wealthier and financially more at ease.

The chief economic advisor at Lloyds Bank argues that it is a fallacy to assume that soaring house prices will cause prices elsewhere in the economy to turn up sharply. If anything, *the RPI plays down the impact of soaring house prices on the average household budget.*

There are many good reasons why house prices are now on a rising curve. As people get richer they can afford bigger and better homes, putting upward pressure on a fairly static housing stock. The 1980s have also seen a revolution in the financial services sector, with increased competition between banks, building societies and other lenders making credit easier to obtain. Two-thirds of all the money on loan from building societies was granted in the last five years. House prices are going through the roof because money has been too plentiful and too cheap for too long.

In 1982, the average house cost three times what the average man earned, or the equivalent in today's terms of £37 000. In 1988, it costs £60 000, or nearly five times average earnings. Like any other speculative bubble, the housing boom will result in a serious misallocation of national resources. *House price inflation eventually feeds through the rest of the economy, both into general consumption and to the labour market.* It would be nice to slow the housing market down greatly but the chances are slim. The bigger the bubble is allowed to get, the louder the bang when it eventually bursts. *Even if house prices just stand still, those with larger mortgages will feel the pinch.*

Chapter Seven

Problems and prospects

'The Cat only grinned when it saw Alice .... "Would you tell me, please, which way I ought to go from here?" "That depends a good deal on where you want to get to," said the Cat.' Lewis Carroll, *Alice's Adventures in Wonderland, 1865*

The Welfare State is mid-way through its fifth decade. For the first two decades its progress went relatively unchallenged, as buoyant economic growth and high levels of employment generated the resources necessary to provide the safety net for those otherwise unable to share in growing economic prosperity. In the 1970s, however, the Welfare State entered something of a crisis from which it has yet to emerge. This crisis owes much to increasing influence of the ideas of the **New Right** throughout the decade, an influence culminating in Mrs Thatcher's election victory of 1979.

The New Right philosophy questions the virtues of the Welfare State from a number of perspectives. It argues that:

- The provision of extensive welfare services smothers the initiative and effort of individual citizens, and creates what has variously been described as the 'dependency culture' or the 'Nanny State'.
- History shows that free market economies, in which governments play a minimal role, are the best able to generate sustained growth of incomes and output.
- In the short term, income inequality provides the necessary incentives to effort, thereby creating the conditions for economic growth.
- In the long run, the benefits of growth will *trickle down* to everyone in society – continued economic prosperity will lower unemployment rates, enable pensioners to receive higher pensions, pay for improved health care and education, and so on.
- The provision of services by effective government monopolies (such as the NHS or state schools) both limits consumer choice and leads to inefficiency owing to lack of competition amongst suppliers.
- Public expenditure on welfare has displayed an uncontrollable tendency to rise, thereby imposing increasingly intolerable tax burdens on the population.

Not all social observers share the New Right philosophy. However, virtually all accept that a crisis in the Welfare State does exist, and there are probably as many views on how to resolve the crisis as there are observers! We shall examine some of these views towards the end of this chapter but, before so doing, we need to add some final details to our picture of the Welfare State in the UK.

The regional dimension

The discussion so far has concerned the efficiency and equity aspects of the Welfare State at the national level. However, analysis at this level hides the fact that the Welfare State impacts upon the lives of the inhabitants of different areas of the country in different ways. This is because economic, social and cultural conditions vary from one part of the country to the next. The incidence of unemployment, for example, shows a marked regional bias, being more pronounced in those areas of the country where large-scale heavy industry has been in decline for over a decade. Thus, the present unemployment rate in Northern Ireland is twice that of Wales and more than three times that of the South East, and this is reflected in the amount of income support paid out to claimants in each region. Figure 22 displays the average annual amount of income support received by individuals in each of eleven regions of the country, demonstrating the diminished relative importance of unemployment in the south and east of the country.

Table 5 provides other illustrations of the differential use and influence of the Welfare State amongst the regions:

- Some areas, it appears, have a higher proportion of local authority housing than do others, reflecting the balance between public and private sectors of house-building programmes of the past.
- Some regions have proportionately more children in state nursery education or staying on at school after the school leaving age, reflecting both local authority policy towards education provision and, perhaps, different traditions as regards furthering one's education.
- The regularity of consulting one's GP also shows a regional variation, in some degree a product of differential patterns of illness across regions.
- Table 5 also displays average annual cash payouts by region for a number of social security benefits other than income support. We see, for example, that the average payout on disability benefit in the North is twice that of Northern Ireland (presumably reflecting a higher incidence of disability), and that the highest pension payout is in the South West (owing to that region's comparatively elderly population.)

Scotland
164

Northern
Ireland
215

North
164

Yorkshire
& Humberside
136

North
West
168

East
Midlands
118

West
Midlands
151

East Anglia
85

Wales
151

South East
124

South West
108

UK average = £139

Figure 22 Per capita income support benefits (£)

The increasing cost of welfare

The premises on which the Welfare State was established after the Second World War were actually quite different from circumstances prevailing today. At that time, it was presumed that:

- Full employment of labour and economic growth would be the 'normal' state of affairs. In fact, the 1944 Employment White Paper committed the government to maintaining high and stable employment levels. It was envisaged that this end could be achieved by using the

Table 5 The Welfare State and the regions

	North	Yorks & Humberside	East Midlands	East Anglia	South East	South West	West Midlands	North West	Wales	Scotland
Proportion (%) of:										
Housing stock rented from local authorities	30	25	20	18	20	15	25	23	20	42
Population consulting GP in previous fortnight	16	16	14	11	14	13	14	15	16	16
Under-fives in local authority nurseries	15.5	16.9	20.7	25.3	23.7	25.4	18.8	19.7	17.7	19.4
16-year-olds remaining in education	60.0	62.4	65.8	59.8	59.8	60.9	61.9	64.7	63.1	76.8
Government spending on cash benefits (£ per head)										
Retirement pensions	329	341	321	337	349	385	307	342	311	309
Sickness/invalidity benefit	93	77	58	35	42	49	62	82	111	91
Unemployment benefit	30	20	16	17	15	20	17	22	25	31
Disability benefit	17	10	7	7	5	5	9	10	13	8

Source: *Regional Trends* 26, Central Statistical Office, 1991

macroeconomic management techniques advocated by Keynes – i.e. increased government spending to counteract a slump in the economy, and deflationary measures to counteract a boom.

- Each individual would therefore 'normally' be working, although short-term unemployment owing to sickness or redundancy could naturally occur. Contributory National Insurance would enable individuals to protect themselves against such eventualities.
- The long period of 'normal' employment during individuals' working lives would enable them to make adequate provision for their old age via the contributory pension scheme.
- Once the backlog of sickness had worked through in the short run, health care spending would stabilize, as the working population grew richer and healthier.
- With the maintenance of full employment, the numbers of those unable to participate actively in the economy would be correspondingly small. This minority could easily be supported by cash transfers from the majority growing increasingly rich.

In recent years, the UK has departed from these early presumptions, most dramatically with respect to the changing incidence of **unemployment**. The average unemployment rate for the period 1951–67 (approximately the first two decades of the Welfare State) was 1.7 per cent, and in no year was it higher than 2.5 per cent. During the 1970s, annual rates gradually rose into the 3–5 per cent range but, since the late-1970s, unemployment rates have paralleled those of the Great Depression of the 1930s (at times, well into 'double figures'). The lowest rate recently achieved (5.8 per cent in 1990) is still over three times the average rate for the 1950s and 1960s. Increasing unemployment poses distinct problems for the Welfare State as constructed in the UK:

- There now exists a far larger sub-set of the population for whom unemployment becomes 'normal', and such individuals are unable to establish a National Insurance contribution record. They must therefore be supported from government benefits financed from tax revenues, rather than from their own contributions.
- Growing unemployment is costly to the Exchequer as well as to the economy as a whole. A person earning £10 000 each year would be producing goods to this value and contributing, perhaps, £3000 in income tax. When unemployed, he or she would receive state benefits of, say, £2000 each year. The economy therefore loses £10 000 in goods produced and the net cost to the Exchequer is £5000. In the UK at present, the net cost of benefits paid and tax revenues lost as a result of unemployment amounts to around £600 per worker.

The maintenance of unemployment is clearly expensive from the state's point of view. However, there is no shortage of additional claims for shares in contemporary Welfare State spending, as we have seen in earlier chapters of this book:

- The demand for **health care**, for example, has proved to be almost limitless (Chapter 5).
- The sale of public sector housing has lengthened waiting lists for such property, and **homelessness** is on the increase (Chapter 6)
- Rapid technological change and the need to maintain industrial competitiveness has led to renewed calls on the government to improve the quality of **education** and training (Chapter 4).
- A problem looming in the near future is the so-called **pensions time-bomb**. As we saw in Chapter 3, the UK state pension scheme is 'pay-as-you-go'. In 1975, a new pension scheme was introduced, requiring higher premium payments but promising higher future benefits. Payouts under this scheme are scheduled to begin towards the end of the 1990s. As this time-bomb explodes, so to speak, the government will have to find a method of generating more money to pay the new pensioners at the higher rates. A complicating factor here is the fact that, as a result of progressive increases in life expectancy over time and a slowing down of the birth rate, the UK population is ageing. The current UK population projections, illustrated in Figure 23, predict a decline in the proportion of persons of school age (those under 16 years of age), but a considerable rise in the proportion of those who have reached the age of retirement (65 years for males, 60 for females). We shall therefore be entering the twenty-first century with a growing number of pensioners dependent for their benefits on the contributions paid by a declining number of working individuals.

Can we afford the Welfare State?

Faced with increasing welfare bills, governments are confronted with a choice between two options. The solution adopted in the earlier part of the Welfare State's history was gradually to raise revenue in line with increasing costs, via taxation, borrowing and National Insurance contributions. However, economic pressures and a different political philosophy led the governments of the 1980s towards the second alternative, namely, the control of costs.

The costs of the Welfare State can be controlled or reduced in a variety of ways:

- *By lowering the real value of cash benefits*. In the early 1980s, for example, the customary up-rating of the value of all benefits in line

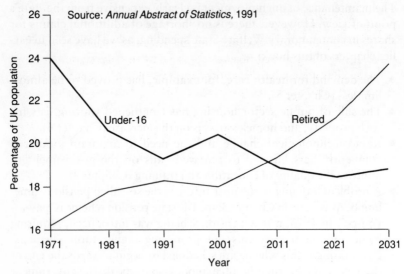

Figure 23 The ageing UK population

with wage or price increases (whichever was the greater) was over-ridden. Automatic up-rating was abandoned for a time, although the government has recently committed itself to up-rating by the rate of inflation (typically less than the rate of increase of wages). Also in the early 1980s, benefits to the young unemployed became age-related, leading to an absolute reduction in the level of benefit for some age-groups. In 1982, the earnings-related additions to sickness and unemployment benefit available earlier were abolished and, in 1985, the value of benefits promised by the 1975 pensions scheme were revised downwards.

- *By increases in **user charges**.* Patients now have to contribute more to, for example, the costs of NHS prescriptions and courses of dental treatment. Between 1979 and 1986, the real cost to the patient of the former quintupled, and that of the latter doubled.
- *By the contraction of the **capital investment programme*** – for example, a slow-down in public house-building and reductions in the maintenance budgets of schools and hospitals.
- *By **privatization*** – i.e. the transfer of service provision from the public to the private sector, entailing the transfer of costs from the taxpayer to the consumer (e.g. the privatization of the NHS optical service in 1986). The government has also **contracted-out** aspects of service provision, in the expectation that competitive tendering for contracts will produce efficiency gains. Examples include the provi-

sion of catering and cleaning services in schools, hospitals and other public buildings.

- *By placing increased reliance on the **voluntary sector**.* Examples include hostels for the homeless operated by the Salvation Army and financed by charitable donations, and tax relief to encourage households to care for elderly relatives at home rather than place them in local authority accommodation.
- *For the longer term, citizens can be encouraged to make their own welfare provision* in the private sector. The 1985 Social Security Act, for example, provided incentives for individuals to leave the state pension scheme and to enter schemes operated by private companies. Throughout the 1980s, there has been a rapid growth in private nursing homes and residential homes for the elderly, with the intention of diminishing the responsibilities of the public sector in these respects.

The problems confronted by the UK governments over the past decade have not been unique – many economies have been experiencing increased demands on welfare spending for broadly similar reasons. As can be seen from the accompanying extract from the *Daily Mail*, New Zealand's response to the problem was strangely reminiscent of that of the UK.

Can we afford the alternative?

Reducing the scope of the Welfare State appears to be the solution to the funding crisis adopted in the UK over the past decade, giving rise, as we saw in Chapter 3, to a marked increase in income equality. The New Right philosophy can legitimate this as a transitory phenomenon, necessary for the economy to retain its strength, after which time the **trickle-down effect** will begin to operate. Sir Keith Joseph, an influential

---

A woman puts the brake on the world's first welfare state

The world's first welfare state was slashed yesterday in "the mother of all budgets". New Zealand's Finance Minister Ruth Richardson, a Thatcher-style monetarist, said there was no alternative to cuts. The massive budget deficit had to be reduced and the economy kick-started into action. She cut government spending, reintroduced hated means tests, scaled down pension benefits, raised health charges, reshaped housing aid and invited private buyers to take over the £358 billion state mortgage scheme.

Historians regard New Zealand as the first welfare state, with cradle-to-grave benefits introduced during the Great Depression in the 1930s. The minister promised "the mother of all budgets" to fulfil the ruling National Party's election promise to produce a budget surplus by the end of its three-year term. Pension entitlements now available at 60 will be gradually delayed until 65 and, for the first time, upper and middle income patients will have to pay a portion of their hospital bills. Prescription charges and fees for doctors' visits will rise, but subsidies for the poor will go up. Higher education fees will be reduced but replaced by means testing which will oblige some students to pay up to four times the old fees. The minister admitted that her party's election promise to halve the unemployment rate was now a dream.

Source: *Daily Mail*, 31 July 1991

New Rightist of the 1970s, preferred the metaphor of all boats ultimately being lifted by the rising tide of affluence.

Economics being what it is, however, we can just as easily develop a case to support the view that this reduction in the scope of the Welfare State itself imposes costs which would be better avoided. Keynes' *General Theory*, for example, argues that richer people tend to allocate a proportionately larger share of their incomes to wealth creation – principally savings, insurance and, nowadays, house purchase. Such monies therefore leak out of the circular flow of income and expenditure. By contrast, the poor tend to devote most of their money to consumption, in order to purchase the necessities of life. It accordingly follows that an increase in income inequality – with the rich becoming richer and the poor becoming poorer – can be expected to depress aggregate consumption and, with it, the entire economy. Put the other way around, higher levels of transfers from rich to poor could be expected to stimulate the economy, presumably to the benefit of all concerned. Keynes himself was strongly opposed to the earlier belief (also held by the New Right) that income inequality was necessary in society, in order that the rich might save funds in order to invest. He pointed out that, without the buoyant consumer demand which could be facilitated by a 'richer poor', no incentive to invest on the part of the rich would exist.

Not all countries during the 1980s pursued policies aimed at reducing the scope of the Welfare State. David Donnison, a professor at the University of Glasgow (and author of the accompanying extract 'Sinking with the tide'), argues that market economies are creating a **'new poverty'**, with characteristics and causes different from the 'old'. Moreover, he argues, the policies being pursued in the UK are actually contributing to the problem and are creating an inequitable and divisive social structure, in contrast to the more equitable policies pursued elsewhere.

Finally, one must be wary of making the automatic assumption that the privatization of welfare services will inevitably produce either equitable or more efficient solutions. There exist no hard and fast economic theories to demonstrate the necessary superiority of private provision over public, or vice versa. A tightly controlled public enterprise may well be more efficient than a private sector firm, in terms of delivering the service at least cost, especially if the latter can exert a degree of monopoly power. Even if services are turned over to the private sector, resources may still be required for **performance monitoring**, as the accompanying extract from the *Observer* demonstrates.

Sinking with the tide

We should recognise that big changes are going on in the richer countries of the world. The long-run tendency of capitalism to equalise incomes has been reversed. during the last 15 years a new kind of poverty has been emerging. The old life-cycle patterns of poverty afflicted most working-class people at predictable stages of their lives – in childhood, early parenthood and old age. Life was tough, but they were not excluded from the mainstream of their society or politically powerless. The new poverty excludes from the mainstream of their society a diverse mixture of groups: middle-aged men whose factories have closed, youngsters who never got a proper job, low-paid workers in marginal jobs, lone parents caring for young children, people who have spent long periods in institutions of various kinds – not a mobilisable political force.

Some countries have tried to check these divisive trends. They keep people in jobs, gain public support for incomes policies which prevent earnings from becoming too unequal, prevent the growth of poverty-striken ghettos in their cities, and use social benefits and taxes to help the poor at the expense of the rich. Britain has followed the opposite strategy. We have allowed unemployment to rise, using it as the main device for managing our economy – "a price well worth paying", as the Chancellor said. Our housing and "urban" policies have divided rich from poor and trapped many of the poorest in ghettos which makes it harder for them to find their way back to the mainstream. Changes in benefits and taxes have taken most from the poorest half of our people and given most to the richer half. As a result, we experienced during the eighties a more savage increase in inequality than any other EC country.

Source: *Guardian*, 21 August 1991

Nursing homes fraud costs DSS millions

The Department of Social Security is being cheated of millions of pounds by private nursing homes who are fraudulently claiming benefits designed to help the dying. Nursing home owners can claim an extra £20 a week Terminally Ill Allowance for residents on income support. But they do not have to prove the resident is terminally ill, and GPs are worried that over-charging is rampant. According to DSS figures, a third of Britain's 70,583 nursing home residents have the extra allowance paid towards their care, at a cost of nearly £25 million a year. The proportion of old people for whom nursing home owners successfully claim has shot up – from 5 per cent in 1986 to 33 per cent last year. A Ministry spokesman would only concede that the figures are "interesting". In some regions the figure is close to 90 per cent. . . . The DSS defines terminally ill, under regulations introduced in 1985, as "having a reasonable life expectancy of six months or less", but some nursing homes have successfully claimed the allowance for residents for up to five years. . . . "The situation is being monitored" [said the spokesman].

Source: *Observer*, 21 July 1991

Where do we want to get to?

The astute reader will have noticed that very few comparisons between the UK and other industrial countries have been made in this book. Such comparisons actually tell us very little, because of the very wide differences in resource endowment, industrial structure, political ideology and popular culture between economies. Suffice it to say that Sweden and the USA are two of the very richest nations in the world in per capita income terms – both are considerably richer than the UK. The former devotes a far greater proportion of its resources to welfare provision than does the UK, whilst the latter devotes very much less. *No explicable correlation between the economic prosperity of countries and the extent of their state welfare provision has ever been devised.*

By way of conclusion, two points made earlier require reiteration. First, in the opening chapters of this book we interpreted the Welfare State as a response on the part of government to perceived efficiency and equity failures in the functioning of the market economy. It accordingly follows that one of the best ways of resolving the crisis in the Welfare State is to eliminate the circumstances which make the Welfare State necessary. In the UK case, it is evident that the funding crisis would be greatly eased were the economy to replicate the presumptions of the post-war model elaborated earlier, by moving nearer to **full employment**. Consider the following simple numerical example.

Suppose we have an economy comprising 80 people producing goods to the value of (and thus earning) £100 per week. Total output is thus valued at £8000. Another 20 are unemployed and need to receive £20 per week in cash benefits. Taxing the employed at 5 per cent will produce the revenue necessary to support the unemployed, and output per head per week for the entire economy is thus £80. If, however, we could engineer an output and employment increase from 80 to 90 people, total output would be valued at £9000. To support the 10 unemployed at £20 per week, we should only need to take £2.2 from each of the 90 wage-earners (a tax rate of 2.2 per cent), and output per head would be £90 per head per week. By increasing employment we have:

- raised average incomes;
- reduced the total cost of cash benefits;
- reduced the tax contribution of each employed person.

Alternatively, higher levels of unemployment benefit (and, for that matter, other benefits) could be afforded at the existing tax rate. In either case, the extent of poverty is alleviated.

The second concluding point is that, as the operations of the Welfare State are the direct responsibilities of government, it is ultimately the electorate in any democracy which determines the path it takes in the future. The enormous growth in state welfare services in Sweden between 1932 and 1976, for example, can be explained by the fact that the same political party, one openly committed to welfare expansion, was returned to office at every general election during the period. In the

UK, public opinion appears to have been more fluid. In 1945, the Labour party committed itself to establishing the foundations of the Welfare State in its modern form, and was elected into office. On the other hand, the Conservative party in 1979 promised to 'roll back the frontiers of the state', and it too obtained electoral success. Clearly, people get the sort of Welfare State they vote for.

KEY WORDS

New Right	Privatization
Unemployment	Contracted-out
Health care	Voluntary sector
Homelessness	New poverty
Pensions time-bomb	Performance monitoring
User charges	Trickle-down effect
Capital investment programme	Full employment

Reading list

Clark, C. and Layard, R., *UK Unemployment*, Heinemann Educational, 1989.

Hurl, B., Chapter 2 in *Privatization and the Public Sector*, 2nd edn, Heinemann Educational, 1992.

McCarthy, M. (ed), *The New Politics of Welfare*, Macmillan, 1989.

Whitehouse, E., 'The economics of manifestos', *Economic Review*, Sept. 1991.

Essay topics

1. Discuss the economic arguments for reducing the role of the state in the provision of health, education and housing in the UK. (Associated Examining Board, 1985)
2. 'Britain has enjoyed a period of strong economic growth; this should have enabled welfare services to have been expanded.' Comment. (Oxford and Cambridge Schools Examination Board, 1990)
3. 'A reduction in benefits available under the Welfare State is a reasonable price to pay for a further reduction in taxation.' Comment on this view. (Oxford and Cambridge Schools Examination Board, 1988)
4. As an economist, how would you attempt to assess how living standards had altered since 1945? What problems do you foresee in making this assessment? (University of London School Examinations Board, 1990)

5. Is it possible to measure the standard of living precisely? Examine the likely long-run effects on Britain's standard of living of changes in the pattern of public expenditure which have taken place in recent years. (Joint Matriculation Board, 1988)

6. Explain what is meant by the term 'ageing population'. Analyse the economic consequences of an ageing population. (University of London School Examinations Board, 1990)

Data Response Question 6

Income inequality and living standards

The accompanying extract from the *Independent on Sunday* of 3 March 1991 is based on an article by Stephen Jenkins in *Fiscal Studies*. Read the extract and answer the following questions.

1. What factors are said to account for the increasing inequality of incomes'?

2. Do the data presented refute the hypothesis of the trickle-down effect?

3. Would it be sensible, from the economic point of view, to raise the level of benefits and pensions as suggested?

4. Do you agree that more education and training would necessarily assist in reversing the long-term income distribution trends indicated in the article?

Margaret Thatcher's economic miracle was miraculous for only the top 40 per cent of the income distribution

One of the most curious facts about the Thatcher years has been the vast increase in inequality of income. . . . The trend helps to explain why the well-paid loved Margaret Thatcher, and why so many of the working-class poor hated her. The 10 per cent of households with the lowest income . . . saw a fall in average weekly income from £48 a week in 1978 to £42 in 1988 (the figures are expressed in 1986 pounds to eliminate the influence of inflation). The 10 per cent with the highest incomes . . . raised their weekly income from £492 to £745 over the same period. The British economic miracle was miraculous only for the top 40 per cent of the income distribution.

But the figures show that inequality had been increasing, albeit more slowly, under the 1974-79 Labour government. Although the 10 per cent with the lowest income were protected by benefit uprating, so that their weekly income rose from £42 in 1967 to £48 [in 1978], the next two lowest paid groups also had actual falls over the period. Indeed, 30 per cent of the population is no better off or worse off [in 1988] than it was in 1967.

If John Major is serious about a more compassionate society, he is going to have to devote some thought to ways in which the bottom third of the income distribution can participate in the increase in national prosperity. One solution is more generous benefits and pensions, raised in line with earnings rather than prices. But the recent acceleration in inequality does not primarily reflect the cuts in top tax rates or the squeeze on benefits, but more unequal gross pre-tax incomes. This in turn results from the supply and demand of scarce skills and talents and is one of the strong arguments for a new emphasis on education and training.

Index